Table of Contents

MW01172515

Croyalflush Ministry Foundation, Since 2011'活石事工基金会, 始于二零一一年.

The Legacy Christian Education & Reinvented Theology merge with Experimental Applied Physics & Proprietary Economics Science Ministry established Platform for Intellects & Computer Nerds.

The Legacy Christian Education & Reinvented Biblical Genetic Science, the Main Branch of Psycho Science, equipping you to end a Christian Journey.

A Scientific & Mathematical Approach to proof End time, Heaven, and Christianity. Not the least, a Biblical Approach to proof End time, Heaven, and Christianity.

独创的基督徒教育与重译神学结合实验应用物理学与专利经济科学事工创立完平台给知识份子与电脑愣子。

独创的基督教育结合重译圣经基因科学，精神病狂学的主要分支。装备你走完基督徒的道路。

用科学与数学的方法证明末世，天堂与基督教。更不止，用圣经的方法证明末世，天堂与基督教。

Those content in these website belong to Oversea Chinese (Guangxi) Medicine & Mandarin (Hainan) Theology Research Topics. Those Production, Reinvent, Publish or Abuse shall bear the Certain Responsibility or Consequences.

此乃华侨民族(广西)与大华民族(海南)的医学神学文案，如有雷同必追究到底。篡改者承当应当责任。

All original content on these pages is fingerprinted and certified by Digiprove.

Choose according to your Christian Equipped Learning Programs. 依照学习编程选择你的基督徒装备程序。

Medicine Renaissance 医药复兴, Biblical Genetic Science, the Biblical Approach to Learn Christianity 用圣经的方法学习基督教。
 *Anglican i.e. Methodist by John Wesley is equivalent to reformed version of Catholic i.e. Vatican. a.k.a. Evangelical Methodist by Charles Wesley. Alpha to Omega, A to Z. Tree of Life. *Biblical Genetic Science is Medicine, oppose to Biomedical.
Vatican 梵蒂冈 (Post-Buddhism 佛教以后)
 Buddhism i.e. Christian Music as Foundation; Santa vs Zombie

Economy Renaissance 高速经济, Economics Science, the Scientific Approach to Learn Christianity 用科学的方法学习基督教。
 *Fundamentalism i.e. Presbyterian by John Calvin is equivalent to retro version of Eastern Orthodox Christianity. Alpha vs Omega. A to A'. Promised Land. *Christian Science is Pseudo Science, oppose to Applied Physics.
Ministry Foundation 事工基金会 (Post-Islam 回教以后）
 Islam i.e. Christian Science as Foundation; Wizard versus Alien

Industrial Revolution 工业革命, Applied Physics, the Coding Approach to Learn Christianity 用编码的方法学习基督教 。
 *Pentecostal i.e. Baptist by Martin Luther is equivalent to evangelised version of Lutheran. a.k.a. Charismatic by Martin Luther King. Alpha & Omega. Z to A. Eden Garden. *Coding Approach a.k.a. Engineering & Word Science & Artistic i.e. Linguistic Code. *Christian Mathematic is Pyscho Science, oppose to Psychology.
Witnessed Testimonial Event 见证分享会 (Post-Hinduism 印度教以后)
 Hinduism i.e. Christian Mathematics as Foundation Christ vs Satan

Reading Policy 阅读政策

Reading Policy (i.e. The Information Contract Acts)

1. **Devotion to Croyalflush Ministry Foundation**: Instead of Charity, we consider our self as Functional & Solution Oriented Organisation exclusively to served God Ministry in terms, **a. Christian Commission** (Hymn Music Dominance, Information Management), **b. Visionary** (Christian Education, Technology Discovery), **c. Missionary** (Economy Miracles, Economy Science Breakthrough), **d. Milestone** (Theology Reinvention, Crime Disruption Objective). Hence, we are not accepting any Devotion in terms of Monetary forms, instead of that, Courtesy if those Legacy devotion via Author's Church Fellow & Islam Neighbour, Family's Connection, Alumni & Profession Union, Nationalist Network are appreciated. Those Legacy has growth into Copyright as time goes by.

2. **Copyright:** U.S. Copyright Registration Number: TX0009107799, 2022-04-02 & TX0009116908, 2022-01-21 (United States Government Issue), Right and Permission under Claimant LAI Hin Wai. Purchase the Paid Content for free reading, and that is Public Property. According to Information Contract Acts. Those content in these website belong to Scientific & Theology Research Topics. Those Production, Reinvent, Publish or Abuse shall bear the Certain Responsibility or Consequences. The Copyright is certified and belong to Author, non-permit Transfer & Sell beyond Author Family, to achieve for high level confidentiality. The Copyright owner has the alteration and destruction rights, but same time bear the Full Responsibility or Consequences if infringe Law. Alternative, to deny Responsibility Bill is to convert the Copyright to Trademark or Patent or Service Mark, or Mental Abduction Burden.

3. **Legacy:** For Legacy donation you may approach the Admin at Wechat ID: ryanlai78. The Legacy contain Intellectual Property Assets and own it at condition of Fully Redemption of Undisclosed Missions or Contracts else Frozen Assets. Alternative, to deny Obligation of Missions or Contracts Tax is to transfer the Legacy, or Jail Terrorism Burden.

4. **Declaration:** Croyalflush Ministry Foundation and Founder doesn't involve any monetary activities such as Security Investing or Land Property nor any Intellectual Property Copyright Selling except the e-commerce store. We don't written support but ignoring any kind of activities involving Terrorism, Mafia, Organised Conspiracy, Cold War, World War.

5. **Manifest:** Our Reinvented Applied Physics & Christian Education Solution focus on Resolution & Regeneration Information Management, & World Threat, especially Climate Change, Nuclear Ransom, Virus Variant Funding, Conspiracy Terrorism. In Addition, our Proprietary Economic Science & Theology Research focus on Decryption & Reformation of World Economics Miracles, & Economy Conspiracy hiding in Digital Economy, Clean Energy Economy, Rare Earth Economy, Knowledge Economy, Infrastructure Economy.

6. **Finance Sponsorship**: Gift owe to those Reputable Audit Profession i.e. Green Cards, Red Cards, Information Platforms, Ethical Property owner with Active Users Formally Compliment in this Ministry.

Acknowledgement 附言

First, thanks go to a lot of community, friends, fellows and business supported the binding of this book, including those important editors in Wikipedia.com, Youtube.com. Most importantly honour to my Lord, and my family & relatives, especially my mother Kheng and father Richard for continued and hopeless support. In addition, I have to thanks my affiliated church, JB Wesley Methodist, and Kindness Presbyterian, pastors Joshua and members of Church incl. Eagles & Ebenezer Cell Group devotion. I wish all the readers incl. my honourable Psychology Doctor Dr. Chan Teck Ming enjoy and support or join the Ministry of God.

Declares courtesy that any Legacy from Church Fellow & Islam Neighbour, Family's Connection, Alumni & Profession Union, Nationalist Network, and not the least I want to thank every Royals for any foresee accomplishment.

Thanks.

首先，感谢于那些社团, 朋友, 长老和业务对这本装订本的支援，包括那些重要的编辑 Wikipedia.com, Youtube.com. 最要紧的是荣耀我的主、我的家人和亲友，尤其是我的妈妈 Kheng 和爸爸 Richard 的不间断和不奢望的支持。 我也要感谢我附属的教会循道宗卫理公会，与恩慈长老会，牧师 Joshua 和各小组与成员 e.g. Eagles, Ebenezer 的奉献。我希望所有的读者，包括我的荣誉心理医生，曾德明医生，的欣赏和支持或携起加入上帝的事工。

声明感谢任何商业机密来自于教会团契与回教邻居，家庭邦交，校友会与工程师联谊，联邦国网络, 还不止这些，我还要谢谢各皇家对这本书后序的成全。

谢谢。

Best Regards,
'Ryan' Hin Wai, LAI
赖庆威
16th August 2020

About Light Encyclopedia & End World Backup Plan 关于光百科与末世备份计划

Disclaimer: Independent Production, reinvent, disclosure, reproduction not granted.

承诺: 独立制作, 重译, 转载, 翻录必究.

- About Light Encyclopedia & End World Backup Plan 关于光百科与末世备份计划

Abstract: An Analysis from the point of view of Ethnicity, Technology, Religion and Economic. Guidelines escape to heaven.

摘要：从种族, 科技, 宗教与经济观点。逃离上天堂手册。

Preface

A long time since early days the prophecy civilisation of technology, music, religion as well as economic had reached out skirt of sky but without leaving clear records or demonstration to integrated what happening insight. Further, those histories After Christ Calendar was in muted, nothing can trace back what filled up the blank until the risen of United Kingdom 'Buckingham Palace' and Islam. These make a perfect description of what this book all about and rule out the future map of breakthrough.

On major side, the motive to write this book, named as [Light Encyclopedia & End World Backup Plan] , come from the point of view of Crime Key Person Disruption for Climate Change Conspiracy. Progressively, Human Right for Christian Persecution, Peace Union for War Crime, Church Reforming for Social Disorder, and Advanced Theology Application in Real World Issue for Technology Evolution as well as Economic Transformation, not the least, the concerning about the Crime Syndicate and Personal Security, there are Speed Evangelism, Explore Denomination Conflicts, Quran Verification for Religion Unity, Spiritual Equipping for Cult.

Last, accommodate for Advanced Civilisation, there are Authentic Pharmacy to New Age Medicine, Advanced Rocket Science Topics to Pseudo Science reinventing, Food and Music Demography to Humanity Heritage.

These are the reasons summary my intention bringing the good news from high and low to you and your family. I trust, in [Light Encyclopedia & End World Backup Plan] you may find peace, fruitful guidance, for the big uphold of the Lord and all his authentic disciples, to your great way for devout contribution to the kingdom in sky, the Praised 'Promised Land'.

Thanks.

序言

从较早前已有一段长时间，就预示中人类文明附属的科技、音乐、宗教以及经济已可到达天方之外，可却没留下明确的记录或指引对所发生的事情与内幕作总整合。 此外，所谓的基督后日历的记录是在全静音状态，没有任何事情可以追溯与填补空白，直至英国'白金汉宫'和伊斯兰教的兴起。 这些是对这是一本什么样的书的完美诠释，并概括未来蓝图的创举。

言归正传，写这本书的动机，即取名为 [光百科与末世备份计划]，是来自于对犯罪关键人物的瓦解与气候变迁阴谋。接着下去，人权与基督教徒的迫害、和平同盟会与战争罪行，教会归正与社会反秩序，高级神学应用与现实世界中的难题，衍生至科技的发展，经济转型。不只是这些，关注于犯罪组织和个人保安的，有迅速传道，宗派矛盾探索，可兰经考证至宗教合一，邪教属灵装备。

最后，预置高级文明的，有正统药剂至新世纪医学，高级火箭科学客题至伪科学重译，美食与音乐的人口分布至人文遗产。

这些理由概括我的意图，把好消息从高与低带到您和您的家人。 我相信，在[光百科与末世备份计划]里，您会找到和平、丰富果实的引导，为主和所有真实门徒，以虔诚的方式贡献于天空的王国，那被称颂的'应许之地'。

谢谢。

Croyalflush Ministry Founders
'Ryan' Lai Hin Wai, 'Richard' Lai Foo Ong, Thang Siew Kheng
11th August 2020

"I am the vine; you are the branches. If you remain in me and I in you, you will bear much fruit; apart from me you can do nothing. John 15:5

"我就是葡萄树，你们是枝条。那住在我里面、我也在他里面的，他才结出很多果子，因为没有我，你们什么也不能做。约翰福音 15:5

A. Technology Highlights 科技标记

- **Clean Energy Economy Doubts.**
- **Comparison between Fusion, Combustion and Electrodialysis**
- **The Break-in of Electric Car**
- **The Know-how of Electric Car Industry**
- **The conceptual Artificial Gill**
- **Game Theory Formation**
- **From Quantum to Pentecost Highlights**
- **Telecommunication Breakthru Backbone**
- **Military Technology Breakthrough Backbone**
- **Application of Breakthrough Technology & Medicine**
- **Carbonless Combustion**

i. Clean Energy Economy Doubts

Clean energy is high maintenance Electronic Borned. And Electronic Technology had not fully established. The Economy Loading is very high.

Best thing comes as free, good thing comes as cheap. This is how the Economics runs. And that define alot of things. is high maintenance Electronic Borned. And Electronic Technology had not fully established. Best thing comes as free, good thing comes as cheap. This is how the Economics runs. And that define alot of things.

Conversely, Product with Low Economic Load, is valuable. e.g. Gold. And the Half life Products, Consumer Products, is High Economic Load.

Now we have Fully Electric Car. The Half life cannot compete with Petroleum Car. For reason of Electronic System Required High Maintenance. Short Half Life Index.

kingdom of heaven is like the owner of a house who brings out of his storeroom new treasures as well as old." Matthew 13:52

As most of us know, Once Energy can be stored, it become none commodity. This is biased toward Business Monopoly. Perhaps stir a war. We cannot store energy, nuclear power is fictional story. And the blockchain of nuclear power incl. Rare Earth hungry Batteries. Data Science useless in this sense, it made excuse. Its called Clean Energy Conspiracy.

Material pollution is okay, but Mind pollution is serious. e.g. Law Disorder. NASA would say, Climate Ecology disorder due to Carbon is the culprit. Carbon Particle is the bottom stream in Organic products. Its time dependent product.

By Chaos Theory, Carbon Particle is reversible. The Crucial is Time Frame. In which linked to Ecology Activities, incl. Law Disorder. Human Population Activities as important as Environment Ecology. Called Time Frames. Carbon is the Culprit. It cause Imbalance of Ecology. Both, Human Economics Activities and Rohs Carbon is equally important for Climate. Control these two, control Climate.

Diesel Car and Petroleum Car not Environment Compliance. Electric power is the option. Rare Earth would became as precious as Gold. And Nuclear Weapon Treaty is high seek after. The Climate Change is based on String of Nuclear Treaty to North Korea. Rare Earth Economics, a.k.a. World War Conspiracy.

Chinese must awakening. Must understand Illegit Finance Activities. Rare Earth would make China become Modernised. Foresee, Open China Policy is dispute because of Culture. Alternative Route is via Data Science and back to Petroleum. I would say concurrently.

For Common understanding, Nuclear Weapon is for Heritage Reservation. The Old Land and Realm. Let's us pray..

What do you worrying about. Climate Change is majority due to Law Disorder. The end of this topics. Let you all to figure out. I like Diesel and Beer, you phew?

ii. Comparison between Fusion, Combustion and Electrodialysis

GLOBAL SEISMIC HAZARD MAP

Figure 1 Global Seismic Hazard Map

A. Applied Physics, Mechanical, Biblical, Game Theory (6per)
Fluorescent Light, Economic Science (Law Inclined), Pro Semitic (Fundamentalist/Atheism, Pre-baptism Agnostic), Shia Islam
Power depend on Public Usage, Nuclear Fusion (Solar Energy: Helium, Chromium)
Benchmark Fuel – No Availability
Reactor (Operation Management) – Safety
Nuclear Waste issue: Ocean Pollution, Biology Disruption (Virus Flu)
Climate Change: **Economic Crisis i.e. Erotic error caused Tsunami**

B. Medicine, Electrical, Pentecost, Actuary Science (5per)
Tungsten Light, Pseudo Science (Waste Inclined), Pro Chinese (Vatican/Episcopal, Post-baptism Multi-theism), Tibetan Buddhism
Constantly Drain Power, Organic Combustion (Organic Energy: Biowaste, Crude Oil, Palm Oil)
Hybrid Fuel – No Clean
Engine (Concurrent Engineering) – Functionality
Carbon Emission issue: Ecology Imbalanced, Physiology Disruption (Oncology Disease)
Global Warming: **Ozone Deteriorating i.e. Ethic error caused Earth Quake**

C. Psyco Science, Electronics, Quantum, Moore's Law (4per)
LED Light, Christian Science (Time Inclined), Pro Egyptian (Evolutionary/Protestant Christianity, Holy Baptism Trinit-ism), Pentecostal 3rd Wave or 4th Wave
Low Efficiency Power, Chemical Electrodialysis (Stored Energy: Battery, Windmill, Hydro)
Metric Fuel – No Cheap
Motor (Quality Management) – Productivity
EMI Electromagnetic Wave Interference issue: Mind Pollution, Veterinary Disruption (Germ Epidermic)
Industrial Revolution: **Rare Earth Wrestling i.e. Food error caused Racial Riot**

French-Jew-Semitic-**Mongolia** high erotic IQ
Mafia activities i.e. Unjustified Sin -Virus
(Hongkong/Malaysia/Taiwan/Singapore)

Germans-Jude-**Mediterranean**-Chinese high ethic CQ
Organised activities i.e. Dishonoured Thief-Tsunami
(Indonesia/Thailand/Malaysia/Guangxi)

Germanic-Jewish-Himalayan-East Asian high patience EQ
Cult activities i.e. Served Evil -Earth Quake (New Zealand/Ukraine/Australia/Germany)

iii. The Break-in of Electric Car

Nuclear Powered
For Climate Change, You have to win over the Economic Crisis and second you have to win over the Alternative Energy. Economic Performance world wide is performance over growth as Education Credential is like wild fire. 2nd, the Nuclear Powered is just a simple decision making of who buy the bill of Ocean Pollution and Humanity Heritage Reservation and most important the Justice and Human Right issue must overcome by just.

Cult activities
This is not easy, no one will buy the shit of Cult Activities who perform the Dark Magic and Colony Slave system. This the Medicine Issue as well as Religion Issue, we shall bring it up. Brute Force is against the Human Right and Justice. There is no place for peace.

Electronic Technology Maturity
To proceed with Clean Energy we need bring it up World Wide and Debate. Who buy the bill? Further, The Electronic Technology Maturity and Precision Technology not reach Maturity yet. By the Clean Energy is a Economic Conspiracy until Present Now 2022', Money drained Machine with no Profitable.

Censored and Quarantine
I am under threatening by Brute force in my Country. I am just an engineer, musician and blog writer. They (FBI) are brute force censored and quarantine my writing, music, and social. When there is no Justice and Human Right, there isn't Church but Cult. Red Card for you. This is my warning to UN. You are wasting your time and money doing Cult Activities. This is my job to wake you up, or War.

Human Right
So you know Human Right? United States Human Right was abolished by Martin Luther King, correct me if I am wrong. A group of Capitalist and a Bankruptcy called Human Right. And this is Democracy in which Objection dominant by Voices.

Oriental Democracy versus Western Democracy
There are Oriental Democracy which dominant by Communist. No Every Voices counted. This is Western Democracy same to Western Nationalism. Check it out. Zero Carbon Emission is Climate Change treaty. Reject this is Start War. But crucial is the timing of this treaty.

Break-in of Alternative Energy
We are yet to right to announce End World Climate, it is reversible, how much you bet? We are to improve the Climate until the Advent of Jesus. We need a wise break-in of Alternative Energy, with abundant allowance. That solely depend on the Maturity of this Civilisation especially the Medicine. In which all technology based on it as Pillar. Depend on your wrist, 'Steel Wrist' Politic is condemn.

Passport to Oriental

5 Standard before the Break-in of Next Phase. 1. World Threat i.e. Economic Conspiracy. 2. World Issue (Erotic Defect & Ethical error) i.e. World War and Cold War readiness. 3. Economic Crisis and Climate Change 4. Intelligence Abuse as well as Terrorism and Religion. 5. Medicine Maturity in which the Technology Pillar. 6. Religion Unity, Israel-Palestine and Silk Road Thai Peninsular. 7. Spiritual War, Speed Church Reformation This is the item of the passport to oriental. And the Judgement done within the Offender.

Brute Force Disrupt Social Structure

Life is a box of Chocolate. Badge. I am going to eat Nasi Lemak Lobster RM35. My job is to resolution, not to disruption. I meant we are progressive harvesting to Next Phase of Civilisation soon. The ball is drop into Malaysian Islam, Chinese and Christianity. This is demographic also the Social Structure. Its fragile.

Climate Change, Constitution Law and Ecology

Climate Change is about Constitution Law more than Ecology. As Ecology imbalance is on the Ozone Global Warming. The Constitution Law i.e. Economics is about the Tsunami. Case by Case. Hard Truth attract no one, but Debating is welcome.

Politics Schism every country so as United States

American Unity is a bubble always. There were mass genocide and mass quarantine and abduction. This is the fact we need to recovered. Stop terrorism topics, the motive has floated. Its evil not righteous. Stupid doo. For there is misunderstanding, there is War. There is schism every country. This is the sign of Devil coming. You are algorithm under developed, indeed.

Extended to Christian Persecution

This is Christian norms of these decades. Turkey in the straw anyone? This is the faulty of Music. The Blues of 50s has censored. Its because Martin Luther King Jr Campaign. Revert the Human Right Doctrine. Its spread like wild fire until present decade. The corner stone of United States has been disrupted. How about other place? Taiwan? This is the religious movement and Christian persecution is the blockchain. We should back to track like ever before and to the church as well. No more Illegal Pentecostal Church funding for whatever sake. Continued like these, we will defer the timelines of civilisation.

Electric Car and Tesla

Its about the Human Genetic Quality. Yoast. Tesla is the father of Electric Car, and for sharp eye this is New Noah. Statement to Electric Car is "Waiting is the beginning of Ageing". Concurrent engineering is not adopted by Japan. This is the Six Sigma versus Cost Efficiency. The manufacturer in Japan earns Trade Secret Credential. The manufacturer in United States earn Cash Interest. Japan firms growth their Factories for Quality Unity. And United States firms doing outsourcing for Cash Efficiency. Tesla technology indeed a Japanese Trade Secret.

Spiritual War indeed
Pay me to shut my mouth out. This is spiritual war indeed, Man versus Creature, China and Taiwan all fallen. All Chinese fallen. Left out Russia, United Kingdom, Germany dominated Europe and Islam Country. I meant Economically which is spiritually.

Religious Movement
Called Religious Movement. Pentecost 3rd Wave, after Martin Luther King Jr. Stop hard words. Some are half creature half man. Let's music do the magic. Please don't censored good music. So as Good looking face. For There is Religion Denomination Dispute or Ethnic Dispute. Christian Persecution vs Anti Semitic. Unfortunate, epidermic could worsen the conflict, and we need to balance the Human Right of Nationalism and Human Right of Communism. Human of Communism form up by Martin Luther King Jr. Human Right of Nationalism form up by Sun Yat Sen 3 People Principles. All run in vain now. there you go, Taiwan implement Same Sex Marriage Law Last few years ago. I am either wing, I support weaker. Right to said Anti Semitic justified Human Right has been abolished.

Spiritual Equilibrium
There is equilibrium point, there is Christian Salt. Don't worry. but Law is Law. Marriage Law affect the Economic as well as the Tsunami and Typhoon. Of course, this is geographical dependent, none of my business. For example, United States Land is liberal land, good weather all the times. All these thing belong to "Oriental Blueprint". And we need break-in ASAP else becomes genetic Yoast. End of Awakening.

Good energy and Bad energy
What is energy? Its come from disruption. So there are Good energy and Bad energy. Of course we need to get the Big Picture. people called Meta. I called it Blueprint. We have collected sufficient informatic of crime activities during 60s to 2022' present. The Final Answer: Anti Semitic and Anti Christ. Recently Anti God. This is fine, Okay!! But War Crime is no tolerated. Nuclear Weapon is disputed so far. But Nuclear Conspiracy is condemned. No one worship. No one worship Nuclear Weapon. This is Psychology. Psychology illness. I would conclude, the Dark Economics is come from Fallen of Morality. Which is Economic Conspiracy. And disruption is via Capitalist e.g. World Bank. Long winner. This is called Obama Economics. Pinned. Ante before Judgement. Its whole stacks of life.

Obama Economics the Economy Conspiracy
If and only disrupt Obama Economics i.e. Capitalism Marketing Economics by Legacy oriented instead of Credential oriented. Evaluation economics instead of Benchmark economics. Metric versus Quantum. Metric Energy is Cubic. Quantum Energy is Hybrid. Crude Oil is Metric. Nuclear is Quantum, in which depend on Weather. Yes The Heat dissipating of Quantum Energy counted into Global Warming. Demographic crucial to Capitalism Economics. Where is your judgemental sound?

Brute Force

Win Moral win War. Seriously condemn Brute Force. In any circumstances, Brute Force required Training. Brute force is last resort. A Science without experimental is full of bullshit. I shall say, when there is brute force there is war. To victory we need Bible combine Quran. Dare to read? There is risk. I am embedded these two in my memories.

Bad things addressed

As Executive Officer, I confess to be the pioneer of World Event Journal. All sets, and we are boring. To those inferior, we had win over the dead and disease, literally. World is going brighter and brighten along the way. The bad things had all addressed. Just enjoy the weekend. Bye for now.

Social Security

Call of duty. War is like Racing of 6 horses. There are white horse and dark horse. Opportunities not equal. But this is Social Hierarchy of God, called Social Bonding. You get Bonding you loss Security. Relatively. This is mathematics, Social Science. To buy security is an offence. In which Social Bonding is Economics and Life. This is because Semitic and Egyptian derivatives is God Election.

Classic versus Popular

The Bible and Quran. Hence, Semitic is Majority, and Germans is Minority. Classic versus Popular. Those middle Class is Semitic. Same applied to Chinese.

Cold War since 60s

Four Economics Premises, and Main Land. Its the Pre-Baptism Fundamentalist and Post-Baptism Vatican wrestling. Applied to India main land and Sri Lanka, Thai Peninsular. There were War Crime events since 60s. Islam is immoral. And Fundamentalist are still minority in Chinese. Most Chinese are Music Oriented. Instead of Scientific. You score Music, you win Chinese. Some Asian are expert in Scripting and Coding called Word Science. That is Yoga or Pentecostal Logo or Graphic belong to these area. The War crime between Islam and Buddhism is due to Economic Conspiracy e.g. Rare Earth, and Erotic Culture and Ethical Short sighted. This is the pillar of most western war too.

Economics War

Conclusion the Game Theory of Economics for the sake of Medicine as Technology Pillar is the root cause of World War. Called Economics War. Its about Erotic and Marriage Law Treaty. Of course, comes with the Climate Change. Its 1000 years cycles. Climate Change discrepancy to Global Warming.

Climate Change versus Global Warming

Its about Tsunami and Flood. Global Warming is about Earth quake. Inner core of Earth. And Moon effect is Tsunami. Tsunami is about Gravitational Wave of Moon. The Earth Quake is true End time, about Inner core Earth Heating. Carbon Emission is irrelevant of Tsunami Prevention. Its about Global Warming due to Ozone Deteriorating.

Tsunami is reversible

Tsunami is reversible. Great news. But Earth Quake is not reversible. That make the highlights of Two Era, Quantum Phase and Pentecost Phase.

Electric Car Break-In Guide

As Combustion Car is not Projected, so we can only use Electric Car at full cost. The break-in should be after the Economics Booming i.e. Moon Landing with Man. 1997 Economic Crisis, we should have the guide of Cold War or Advent.

Cold War Crime

That make the blinds of 911 Terrorism. And series of Epidermic along the way. There required only 40 years or 50 years to Oriental. The number is biblical. It is a cycle, present is best bet. 40 years after advent. or Cycle again. Called Silk Road. Myanmar War, Vietnam War, China 64 Protest, Taiwan Strait Tension, Xin Jiang Rehab, Hongkong Extradition Law, etc.

James Dyson the New Noah

The Fundamentalist bind with Vatican and New Age Religion. Its Cruel, better than defer. Last, the 6 Economic Body Game Theory Wrestling in terms of Medicine Pillar for Technology. Called Economics War. Religion War or Christianity Evolution. Another Competitor is Dyson. The New Noah is James Dyson. Electric Floating Technology

Religion the Technology Pillar on Medicine

Genetic Quantum Science is Fundamentalist, Cardiovascular Pseudo Science is Vatican, Psychology Biblical Science is New Age Religion. Its Horse Racing time. "The future cannot be changed but this is not destiny."

Sovereign of God

As we progress into Advanced Civilisation (time slow phase), World War is impossible. The degree of freedom depends on your Holy Spirit. Called Sovereign of God. Fatalism and Pre-destined and Full destined. Colony and Mainstream determine the God Sovereign. This is proof by literacy and educated rate.

Technology War the Religion War the World War

World War III is indeed a technology war. Most of us are full of funs. Word Games or iPad. We ought to ride the Tesla and emitting to Mar. That required good batteries and acceleration. Light of Speed is possible. Just required Gear shift. Pseudo Science, i.e. Statics can make Floating with Electric Supply.

High Volume Fees

Semitic Supremacy thingy. Because of Quantum Technology. The rest pay high volume fees. Another Competitor is Dyson. The New Noah is James Dyson. Electric Floating Technology. We could easily make another version but still within the Statics boundary. Okay, let make Electric Car at full economical cost for Prevent Global Warming and Earth Quake. And it's the most safety car than Combustion due to Manageability of DC. And this is the Electronics Technology in works, called A.I. Holistic Limitation. Spirit mobilised. EMI issue. The Quantum Computer has no reach maturity yet.

High Maintenance

Once again. Its just too early to break-in, despite its Japanese stuff. Six Sigma Quality Management instead of Concurrent Engineering. Those are the common doubts. Electronic machine required high maintenance.

Organised Crime

Let's lit the light. Whole bunch of Organised Crime. This is True Human Right Concerns. Not About Gender equality, not about Same sex marriage, not about Job Wage, not about Neighbourhood Law Suit. Its about our life, past life, present life, future life and after life to eternal life. I got alot of clues and accumulating for filling. Not a big hit, no supposed to. But a Change for better Talk. I believe pass over these messages to next 14 generations, would help. Its completed darkness in my sight. So you can think the Colony are very wide spread. At least Chinese.

Oriental Democracy the rootcause

I can deduce this Far East Countries issue. Because of so called Oriental Democracy. That what the Economics moves. Western is the media of passive. Stop hiding, stand out. Stop disguise yourself. Peace comes at high price. Let's see how, I stand out for now.

iv. The Know-how of Electric Car Industry

Integrity
Integrity is all about to be voices. Or just read the bible. Credential hungry man. You got to raise up one day. I see for spiritual identity. A humble man lead to victory. A proud man leads to self destruction. No one man show. Be the running man. One man show is involuntary. In a War, the most important is the Creed. Its an advanced algorithm. And the winning method is creep. This is the neck guarding. What all about Patience and Holiness is. The Lite.

Semitic vs Semitic
This risk management strategy called Victory theology. Semitic vs Semitic is dead end. We have Penta. So called Anti Tau. Don't be the lajuruk i.e. Last. You are the best I think, due to Vatican against UN. Pro China. Terminator. And that is Cold War.

Censored of Blues Music and Irish
I have my musical senses. The Blues Irish (Fundamentalist Creationism) versus Hymn Anglo (Episcopal AZ) versus Folk Russian (Episcopal Alpha Omega) versus Rock Hebrew (Fundamentalist Calvinism). The Creationism and Intelligent Design has censored.

Fundamentalist French and Calvinism Germany
Because of Washington Apple is for Liberal Land only. This is the important part. Major reason is Jeopardy by Islam. So called Islam Scholar design Car without the needed of experiments. This is from French Fundamentalist. Germany is Fundamentalist Calvinism. The different is Experimental versus Theoretical that is the methodology the invention of 9 page Quantum Computing.

IBM platform and Electric Car
China is the winner. The computation flop is non-limited. Its the right time break in the Electric Car. We had almost to established the Computer Platform. IBM platform. Sound technology is the Crab now. Called Pentecost Science.

Chinese Medicine is Psycho Science, i.e. Artificial Intelligence
Without Computer Platform established, electric car is non economical feasible. The Sound card technology. Psych Science is the Crab. And this is the Patent of Chinese Medicine. Without Pentecost Science without Artificial Intelligence. Chinee Scholar had been abduction in mental rehab because of this.

Background Story of Artificial Intelligence
The behind reason of 911. The truth has floating to me since last year 2021'. Bill Gate is monopoly. Sound Card is the Pillar of Electric Car simply put. Car Audio? Nope. This is the Judgement of Semitic 12 sects. Sometime right sometime wrong. Forgiveness is all about.

Germany the key to Religion Unity

Personal Victory is all about passport to heaven. The story of Semitic has alot. Qualification and Reconciliation is the key. For Authentic is belong to Germanic. The Prague Square vs Jerusalem. The Germany has the best religion Fundamental. So called Authentic. Turkey in the Straw, Religion Unity. Without Germany, Palestine and Israel had no peace.

No Discrimination on Ethnic

Of course alot of Jewish gentile in Israel. Best Ethnic Russian, Best Christian Germanic. Unfortunate, there another Martin, Called Martin Luther King Junior. This makes Moon Landing United States and Challenges and Promises. We can't denied African for the vain efforts. We have to accept them enjoy the Fruit of Economic Booming.

Christian walks out Church

As a results, as Bible Prophesised, Cult Activities Raised. The Dark Magic one. Those devout Christian walks out the Church. As written in the bible commentary. Solar System is constituted by 9 planets, 8.5 to be exact. And the formation of Planet is the scale of the Geometry. There are total 3 kind of formations. This is the Church, Fundamental, Pentecostal and Episcopal. Buddhism Inclined, Islam Inclined and Hinduism Inclined. The combination of Cult and Orthodox.

Unity but Components of a Body

It is not mixture but aligned. Same thing we cannot mix church, but aligned church. we cannot mix ethnic, but align ethnic. and this is complicated task. But no compromised. Migration crisis is a serious problem in Malaysia. One day this will be aligned to each country. Culture, language remain. The Romance of Three Kingdom. United Nations, Promised Land, and Oriental. Same story applied to each nations. One within each one.

Green Green Grass of Home

There are 3 kind of Social Bonding which deduce from Geology. And Economics is Politics, and Politics is Geology. The Geology is the Ethnic. Protect the land is everything than people. Back to the green green grass of home. This is the failure of China because Hongkong and Shanghai was rental premises. And the land determined your money. There is green in every country, don't migrate. But conquer instead. Teach you how.

Japanese way the Levi way

By Electronic Gadget. This is Japanese way. Not Burger King. And Japanese doing no profit business. Due to this reason. Japanese way doing Branding is expanding continuously. Non Profit Business but Rich Citizen, how can? The strategy of growth big. For Levi people doing business this way too. This is doing business the army way. This is complicated accountancy.

China Concurrent engineering versus Japan Quality Management

But the Victory belong to Taiwan, why? Panasonic National. They doing concurrent engineering. Focus on Function per Cost. This is important feature for Electronics. So Japanese make Combustion Car, China make Electric Car. Cool? High Mix low Volume versus Low Mix High Volume Batteries is High End Price, Petroleum is depending on Market Supply. Solar is occasional availability same applied to Nuclear Powered.

Joint Design Manufacturing and Blue Sea Strategy

Which economic is fit to future scenario? Overhead no important but Depreciation rate. Electric Car is Win Win. High Depreciation Half Life (Low Heat Loss), but Expensive Battery. Electric Car is Win Win. Low Depreciation Half Life (Low Heat Loss), but Expensive Battery. Combustion has very lowest efficiency rate. The heat can make use to boiling eggs. So Electric Car is Concurrent Engineering, Joint Design Manufacturing. Most country able to make their own Electric Car. This is Blue Sea Strategy. Multi Channel.

The Contest of Monopoly

To gain Monopoly. The Core Patent. Its a racing contest. Monopoly eliminates unnecessary marketing Economic Conspiracy.

Electric Car the Mercedes Way

The crab of a Car is the Pneumatic or Hydraulic Instrument i.e. Dashboard. This is the core technology of electric car too. The Lubricant. This required off road trial. The Robustness of Electric and the Handling. Doing the Electric Car the Mercedes way. This separate the price tag.

Ethic First

This is about Sport and Skills than Formula. No many Generation expect, just 3 generation enough. Ethic come first Safety second. You have to build a wing if it can fly. Same thing, the electric car must be skills hungry. Cannot man-less or fully automatics. Non ethic.

No Weapon

Ok, there is pollution too, sound pollution. Tinnitus inclined. High Pitch and loud. Interference with IoT 5G. A safety Car indeed. Required Tuning every forth week. or Everyday the best. It can be very miniature, for kids. but non ethic. It is weapon.

Transparency from 5G

It can be. Transparency from 5G. stop here, Because of Global Warming and for the sake of Earth quake in Pacific. We need these break in straight after Religion Peace in Israel. i.e. Entering Silk Road, Pentecost Era.

With Uncertainty of Dispute from Crude Oil Economic Body, we cannot brute force. History condemns. In Quantum Era, 4G Era, we are safe from Global Warming I guarantee. That is differ of Close Form Universe and Open Form Universe.

Prepare Readiness of Electric Car

But Celestial is secret. Humble Telescope James Webb Telescope is Hobbies. Studies Mathematics studied Universe. Not Sketch form Picture. Its financial manipulation schemes. We need safe guard Celestial. We don't know the time of Global Warming, but prepare the readiness of Electric Car is the wise path.

Patience for Booting

So as Nuclear Powered. Semitic Availability. Made for Semitic. Electric Car made for Germanic, know why? You need to have patience waiting booting. Maybe Tuning every time restart. Tuning the Gauge. This will be solved if 5G era. If Driving don't use Handphone. And 5G handphone no safety. and no healthy. Take caution.

v. The conceptual Artificial Gill

Your vocal. Is your Heart Beat. You can't loss your vocal. Its Combustion of Chemistry. Air Supply. There is alternative. Maintain the heart beat. By supply of food energy.

With Food, we can sustain and support life. The Lung is the crab. We can Breath like fish. In Space of Universe or Upper Sky. Or Emergency.
Without this, Fly in the Sky cannot become mainstream. Most important is for Mar explorer.

Without man landing on Mars, we cannot determine True Heaven and True Holy Spirit. Is Jazz Music Good? Is African True Holy Spirit? All these can verify double.

For me, Hell is my heaven. Let's call the thing off.

vi. Game Theory Formation

1. 1D dot matrix i.e. portrait

Figure 2 Dot Matrix

2. 2D sketch, kinematic, cryptography i.e. signature

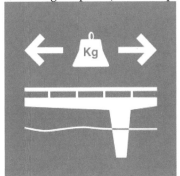

Figure 3 Cryptography

3. 3D statics, loading i.e. photo/ 1 axis is pivot

Figure 4 Static Force Equilibrium

4. 4D 3D+kinematic, film i.e. video/1 axis is pivot

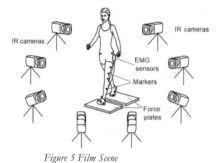

Figure 5 Film Scene

5. 5D 3D vector->parametric, wire flame, chassis, architecture i.e. blueprint/2 parameter is pivot i.e. pillar

Figure 6 Car Chassis

6. 6D parametric kinematics, linkage i.e. moving/2 linkage is pivot i.e. controller

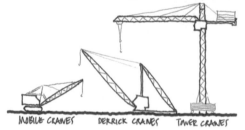

Figure 7 Variety of Crane

7. 7D parametric dynamics, robotic arm, motion i.e. force/tip grounding required i.e. calibration

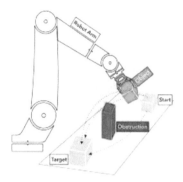

Figure 8 Robotics Arms

8. 8D parametric electromagnetic, motor i.e. momentum/2 phase

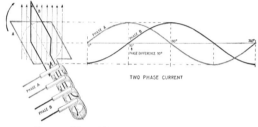

Figure 9 Electro Motor

9. 9D parametric thermodynamics, thermal i.e. heat/2 type of Sequence i.e. 1 Scale

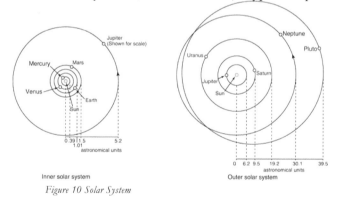

Figure 10 Solar System

10. 10D parametric gravitational, quantum i.e. light/3 type of mode

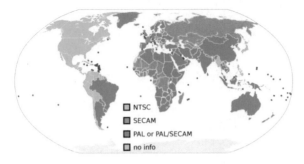

Figure 11 Television Color Mode

11. 11D parametric radiant, pentecost i.e. sound/tip grounding required i.e. tuning

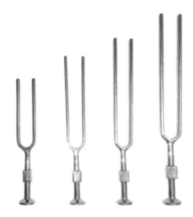

Figure 12 Musical Forks

12. 12D parametric material, digital i.e. electric/2 direction i.e. switch a.k.a. flops

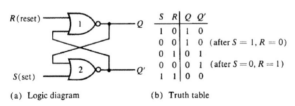

(a) Logic diagram   (b) Truth table

Figure 13 Switch Diagram

vii. From Quantum to Pentecost Highlights

1a. Backbone Printing Press Inventor – Bi Shen, Gutenberg, etc.
Hence the Christianity as well as it brother Fundamentalism Islam may able preach from Prague to Mainstream Population.

Figure 14 Gutenberg Printing Press

1b. The 1st Church Reformation, Binding Creationism and Genesis to Science Class Room – Martin Luther, John Wesley, etc.

Figure 15 The typical Scientific Theology Book

2. Breakthrough of Applied Physics a.k.a. Economic Science – Wright Brothers, etc.
Hence the Promising Democracy, Human Right and Economic Booming bring Advent of New Era to Religion Diplomat Era in Israel and Palestine.

Figure 16 Wright Brothers Airplane Testimony

2b. African Human Right and Preaching Wave from African and South American and to United Nations – Martin Luther King Junior, etc.

Figure 17 Pioneer of African Human Right

3. Telecommunication Economy a.k.a. Economic Science Established – James Webb, James Dyson, Bill Gate, etc.

Hence the Bible and its derivative Books may spread to every corner of World, and there may able for many translations, versions, commentary, geography map and Theology Research Books launched.

Figure 18 United States James Webb Telescope

3b. Semitics Human Right Revolution in Chinese and Western, and the Rise of Fundamentalist Belief in China Mainland, Chinese Economic Premises, and Japan and Islam Communities a.k.a. Islam Renaissance. – Sun Yat Sen, Vladimir Putin etc.

Promote Chinese Economics by Pioneer Technology Automatic Control as well as Martial Arts Jet Kun Do – Bruce Lee, etc.

Figure 19 China Chang Er' 4 Moon Landing

New Moses – New Noah – James (Law) (Economics)
James Dyson->James Webb, Bill Gate
Chinese Noah->Bruce Lee (Hongkong Hollywood, etc)
New Solomon – New Joshua – Martin (Politics)(Religion)
Martin Luther->Martin Luther King Junior
Chinese Joshua->Sun Yat Sen (Nationalist Revolution, etc), Vladimir Putin (Nazi Syndicate Disruption)

viii. Telecommunication Breakthru Backbone

Northern Star 北斗星 (check Organic Stellarisation)->Determine Alpha Omega Timeline by Music scale and Homogenous Genetic (100x5x4 years cycle)
Universe: Solar/Time Phase i.e. Horoscope type->British System; Imperial System; International System->Ethnic i.e. Culture **(Left Wing or Right Wing, Era)**
Music scale 9 type->12 mode i.e. North to South i.e. Lake North or Lake South
Quantum->9 type of Harmony Scale->1 of 9 Scene i.e. **3 Overlapped, Meta Universe, Holistically**, Simulation (2200km Ethnic Polar)
Day->7×4 Quantum typical English Words, and then Formation of Sentences Structure->Formation of Encyclopedia (The Answer and Question).
Broadcast Satellite 4G->Holistic->3×12 Satellite->Optic->TV
James->Jehovah

Tide Wave 潮汐 (check Chemistry reaction time)->Determine Geneva Timing by Radiant Scale and Individual Organic (20x5x4 years cycle)
Galaxy: Star Phase i.e. Calendar type->Islam Calendar, Semitic Calendar, Chinese Calendar->Religionism i.e. Nationalism **(9 Religion Festival, i.e. Economic Activities)**
Radiant Scale 3 type->(14-2)x2 hours i.e. Western or Asia
Pentecost->Percentage of Holy Spirit->24 Spirit i.e. **24 Portion, Remote Identity, Homogeneously**
Year->12 prototype of Other Language Script->Formation of Language Word->Formation of Thesaurus (Light and Salt).
Radar 5G->Homogeneous and Isotype->2 Parallel->Electromagnetic->Radio
Mary->Jesus

Polar Light 火山；嫦娥；大白兔 (check Water Mineral Polarity)->Determine Politics by Gravitational Scale and Holistic Psychology (4x5x4 years cycle)
Planet: Moon phase i.e. Weather type->Economic Crisis; Economic Booming; Economic Conspiracy->Economics i.e. Industry **(6 Perpetual Jobs, i.e. Politics)**
Gravitational Scale 9 type->10 social network i.e. Mount East to Mount West
Biblical->12 type of Typical Biblical Character->1:520 **Rotating, Gentile, Individually** *75Billion/12×12000 Rotating means all can be True, but Virtual Account i.e. Non Active.
Month->5 Major Vowel add 23 Major Consonant, and then the Formation of English Word->Formation of Dictionary (The Reference)
Telescope Radiant 6G->Individual->1 out of 7 kind->Matter Wave->Internet
Christ->Messiah

*2 of 2 Promised Land is Oriental. *1st Promised Land and Devil Gangs get Judge. May able go Fire Lake. *2nd Promised Land, people get Judge. May able go Hell.
*Ethnic decides Advents; Religion decides Salvation population; Economics decides Weather.

ix. Military Technology Breakthrough Backbone

A. Regulator
Heat Flux Fan Control System e.g. Aircraft
Fluid Compressor Control System e.g. Truck
Switch Button Control System e.g. Ship
Military Standard: Active and Autopilot Supplementary Processor Unit.

B. Power Train
Radiant Fusion – Mechanical e.g. Submarine
Organic Combustion – Electrical e.g. Train
Mineral Chemistry – Electronics e.g. Electric Car
Military Standard: Safety from Self Explosion.

C. Mobility
Electromagnetic Motor e.g. Bus
Linkage Mechanism e.g. Bicycle
Automation e.g. Crane
Military Standard: Booster avoid incoming Accident.

D. Telecommunication
Radar Signal – e.g. Tank
Satellite Signal – e.g. Van
Radio Signal – e.g. Motorcycle
Military Standard: Intercept Signal avoid from Trajectory Object.

E. Ergonomics
Crabmachine AI system, Navigator – e.g. Taxi
Meta-Universe VR system, Road Track Feedback – e.g. Drone
Computer Aided AR computer system, Power Trigger – e.g. Lift
Military Standard: Remote Control

x. Application of Breakthrough Technology & Medicine

A. Pioneer Telecommunication Technology Application
- Climate Disaster Prevention and Total Elimination (**Pioneer**)
- Accurate Population Census for Infrastructure Development (**Pioneer**)
- Demographic for Crime Disruption (**Pioneer**)
- Ancient Date Estimation (**1980's**)
- Geographical Location Prediction (**Pioneer**)
- Population Traffic/Logistic Management (**1990's**)
- Mobile Live Camera for Family/Personal Security (**2020's**)
- Online Class Room (**2020's**)

B. Pioneer Military Technology Application
- Air Floating Bicycle (**Pioneer**)
- Dinosaur Truck (**Pioneer**)
- Drone Crane (**Pioneer**)
- Electric Car (**2010's**)
- Passive Crash Control (**Pioneer**)
- Active Crash Control (**2010's**)
- Cloud Taxi (**2020's**)
- Air Floating Train (**2000's**)
- Cloud Air Fighter (**2020's**)

C. Pioneer Medicine Application
- Schizophrenia, Tumour – Sleep Testing & Herbs Stellarisation, Job Treatment (**Pioneer**)
- Epilepsy, Chronic Disease – Skin Testing & Salt, Religion Treatment (**Pioneer**)
- Psychopathic, Virus Infection – Color Blind Testing & Radiant, Music Treatment (**Pioneer**)
- Mineral Water build muscles and hence weight loss. (**Pioneer**)
- Organic Products detoxify, and hence control ageing. (**2000's**)
- Fragrant cleans lungs, and hence fights against Virus. (**Pioneer**)
- Schizophrenia, Tumour – Lumen Sensitivity Testing (**1970's**)
- Epilepsy, Chronic Disease – Tongue Speech Structure Testing (**1910's**)
- Psychopathic, Virus Infection – Hormone Sensitivity Testing (**1970's**)

xi. Carbonless Combustion

Let us find out the Performance of the Combustion using the Distilled Crude Oil.

The choice of Distilled Crude Oil is based on the faith on the 14 derivative generation of Organic Compound shall return to the initial state of purity.

The Carbonless Combustion is based on the faith that the balanced Carbon dioxide exhaustion to the entire Ecology and effect to Ozone deterioration.

First of all, the Performance is measured by the efficiency of the combustion as well as the heat transfer.

The Carbon Chain Structure more complex, the more efficient of the combustion due to the ease of yield of carbon dioxide. vice versa.

The empirical formula for the combustion is

$C-C-C \rightarrow CO^2 + H2O + $ Other Chemistry Compound.

The ease of the combustion is measured by the purity, there are only the Crude Oil and the Ammonia the equivalent highest purity and homogenous characteristic.

Combinedly, the Heat Transfer depends on the Entropy of the Carbon Chain Structure. And it is the Crude Oil first rank and the 14th derivative the Ammonia i.e. last rank equivalent too.

The Entropy Index could measured by the Heat Capacity or Boiling Point.

Possess high Heat Capacity and Boiling Point, the explosive Index shall be lowest, and this is for safety concerns.

Credit to ASME America Society of Mechanical Engineer "Topic, Decarbonizing Engines using Green Ammonia and e-Fuels"

B. Medicine Highlights 医学标记

- **How compare between Biology, Medicine & Veterinary**
- **医学探索之佛教与回教近时代斗争**
- **How to each Ethnic gain wisdom & health?**
- **Medicine Breakthrough Backbone**

i. How compare between Biology, Medicine & Veterinary

Veterinary Science. Its not Medicine but Medical. Surgery is Medical. All these based on Christianity Theology as Foundation.

Three Theology as Foundation, Calvinism Theology (Islam), Arminianism (Buddhism). Anabaptism (New Age).

Calvinism is Save by Faith Alone without Baptism but Pre-baptism. Dependent on Islam Election People incl. Egyptian and Semitic. Christian Science.

Arminianism is Save by Works without Baptism but Post-baptism. Dependent on Buddhism Victory and Placebo effect. Pseudo Science.

Anabaptism is to Salvation by Grace that to Baptise Gentile Spirit to Holy Spirit (5per). Dependent on Grace of Trinity God. Quantum Science.

Psychology is not Medicine but **Optometry** i.e. Eye Science, the Veterinary. Another One, Genetic Science is related to **Orthopedic**. Orthopedic is not Medicine, but Geneology and Biology. Comes to Physiology, that is related to **Cardiology**, Health Science. All of these called Medical.

The Cardiology treatment is nutrition supplement i.e. Topical Paste (skin). The Orthopedic treament is enzyme, i.e. Drug Pills (brain). The Optometry treatment is vitamins i.e. Injection Stemcell (lung).

The true Medicine and Chinese Medicine. Namely, 1. Body (Applied Physics)(Bone Healer), 2. Body and Spirit (Pseudo a.k.a Economics Science)(Herbs), 3. Spirit (Psycho Science a.k.a. Computer Science)(Acupuncture).

ii. 医学探索之佛教与回教近时代斗争

举列佛教与回教的斗争渐渐从七十年代泰国半岛越南战争缅甸战争至今日的新疆改造训练营，罗兴亚人危机，中国六四事件，台湾两岸局势，香港逃犯条约等。

人道危机，人权自由，基督徒迫害，文字狱，宗教自由都是受到西方社会关注的。而其中混杂了，稀土经济阴谋，气候变化阴谋，干净能源阴谋。

而佛教与回教的盼望在于中国的统一，区域与远东国家的和谐。这就是我们所知道的"丝绸之路"，一条高速经济通往东方极乐世界，就是基督教的天堂。

遗憾的是，天堂是个秘密，各国都拼命的掩饰与保持暧昧关系。

这主要有六大经济体之医学博弈，再说一次，医学博弈。称之为医学复兴时代。Medicine Renaissance. 大家都知道，医学研究需要克服经济风暴，气候危机，能源危机等。就证明了，强调经济,法律次序道德上的成功才是医学成功的关键。

#5 Communism 共产党 **(Oriental Democracy 东方民主)**->New Age 新世代宗教 (French->Semitic), Optometry (ENT Disease, Dental)(Environmental Pollution inclined)

#2 Federation 俄联邦 **(Federal Constitutionism 中央立宪)**->Buddhism 佛教 (Jude), Cardiovascular (Acute Disease, Epidermic)(Ethnic Inclined)

#3 Federalism 中央联邦 **(Republicanism 共和)**->Islam 回教 (Jew), Orthopedic (Psyciatric, Migraine)(Crime Inclined)

#4 European Union 欧盟 **(国民主义 Nationalism)**->Islam 回教 (Germany->Semitic), Genetic (Oncology Disease, Leukemia)(Inheritary Inclined)

#1 Capitalism 世界银行 **(Democracy 民主)**->New Age 新世代宗教 (Levi), Psychology (Chronic Disease, Organ Failure)(Allergy inclined)

#6 Commonwealth 英联邦 **(Royal Constitutionism 皇家立宪)**->Buddhism 佛教 (Anglo->Semitic), Physiology (Paediatric, Flu)(Religion Inclined)

iii. How to each Ethnic gain wisdom & health?

United Nations, Communism – Medium Trade Deficit->Medium Economical Returns
Quality Management, **SME Small & Medium Engineering**, GNP, Productivity – Quality & Material Selection
Cambodia, Ukraine, Portuguese, Spain, Jewish & Gentile, Africa, Japan, Mandarin 华夏系 (苏州)
Yoga/Pentecostal/Monotheism, Hinduism, Yoga: Physical Activities (Report, Experiment, Laboratory)
Bone Healthy ->Immunity Proof (Involuntary caution)(Slave tendency, Dog)->5th. Repentance

Diaspora Jews Union, Federation – Largest Trade Deficit->Highest Economical Returns
Concurrent Engineering, **MNC Multi-National Company**, GNP per capita, Individual Productivity – Functionality & Ergonomically
Myanmar, Belarus, France, Russia, Jude & Judah, Turkey, Tokyo, Tiong Hua Diaspora 中华藩属系 (上海)
Zen/Eastern Orthodox/Trinit-ism, Christianity: Ministry Activities (Project, Application, Computer Suit)
Lung Healthy ->Spiritual Proof (Hygienic caution)(Running Tax tendency, Cow)->1st. Righteousness

European Union, Capitalism – Low Trade Deficit->Low Economical Returns
Operation Management, **F&B Food & Beverage**, GNI, Income – Cost Effectiveness & Brand Index
Laos, Poland, Germany, Australia, Irish & Levi, Arab, Gangnam, Putong 普通系 (浙江)
Silk Road/Fundamentalism/Agnostic, Islam: Fasting Month (Thesis, Theory, Library)
Brain Healthy ->Allergy Proof (Voluntary caution)(Violence tendency, Pig)->4th. Forgiveness

United Kingdom Federation, Commonwealth – Large Trade Deficit->High Economical Returns
Federal Regulation Compliance, **PSC Public Service Commission**, GNI per capita, Individual Income – Reliability & Pollution Compliance
Thailand, Greece, Netherland, United Kingdom, Anglo & Semitic, Egypt, Korea, Peking Cantonese 京粤系 (南京)
Tibetan Buddhism/Episcopal/Atheism, Buddhism: Vegetarian (Lecture, Technical, Training Room)
Heart Healthy ->Ageing Proof (Idle caution)(Corruption tendency, Duck)->3rd. Tolerance

Nationalism & Republican, Federalism – Zero Trade Deficit->Zero Economical Returns

Operating Standard Management, **MIS Management Information Systems,** GDP, Profit – Safety & Economically

Vietnam, Romania, Italy, United States, Jew & Canaan, Palestine, North Korea, Oversea Chinese 华侨系 (杭州)

Shaolin Buddhism/Catholic/Multi-theism: Spiritual Activities (Tutorial, Practise, Workshop)

Sex Gland Healthy ->Hormone Proof (Erotic caution)(Erotic tendency, Chicken)->2nd. Holiness

iv. Medicine Breakthrough Backbone

Genetic-Flesh & Muscles->Oncology, (Schizophrenia, Energetic)(causes of Vegetable Death and Suicide Death)
Vitamin-Vaccine (Mineral, Water)->To change Religion type
Quantum i.e. Wave-Particle Duality-Morse Code (Portrait)
711 practical, theoretical, experimental, perfection (Religion type depend on Lover and Era)
Body (Classification): Flesh of Adam (Mineral)+ Rib of Adam (Nutriology)+ Forbidden Fruit (Chemistry), (3 type of **Terrain**)(Himalayan, Mediterranean, Mongolia) i.e. 8 type of **Genetic Behaviour** leveraging flesh and wisdom.

Cardiovascular-Rib & Blood->Physiology, (Epilepsy, Talented)(causes of Sudden Death)
Nutriology-Topical (Organic, Land)->To change Ethnic type
Biblical i.e. Hexagram->Cryptography Code (Vocal)
14 prototype generation (Ethnic type depend on Family and Geography)
Body and Soul (Rating): Dust (9 binder **Continent** of 12 type Geology Botanical Species) i.e. 9 type **Continent Avatar**.

Psychology-Nerves & Joint->Eye Science, (Psychopathic, Extraordinary)(causes of Natural Death)
Enzyme-Drug (Chemistry, Air)->To change Allergy
Pentecost i.e. Analog->Light Code (Skin Tone)
3 type (Allergy type depend on Church i.e. Enemy and Event)
Holy Spirit (Popularity): God Breathed (9 type **Chemistry**)

C. Economics Highlights 经济标记

- **Personal Finance Myth**
- **The Introduction of New Economic System**
- **Colony Slave System**

i. Personal Finance Myth

Church & Management (Dominancy – 1st Rank)
(**Tax or Interest**, Fortune/Nightmare)(Related to Personal Wills) – Gold i.e. Insurance
(In the form of Life Expectancy or Environment Quality) – from United Nations & Federal Bank Forecast Budget

Family & Accounting (Dominancy – 2nd Rank)
(**Main Expenses**, Leisure/Eye Watching)(Related to Identity Census) – Foods & Drinks i.e. Commodity
(In the form of Bill or Raising Fund) – from Government or Union Welfare

Back Stage Role & Finance (Dominancy – 5th Rank)
(**Side Income**, Investment/Job)(Related to Risk Management) – Stock & Crude Oil i.e. Share
(In the form of Hidden Tax Chips or Persistency Compensation) – from Company Profit Sharing

Business & Economics (Dominancy – 4th Rank)
(**Main Income**, Treasure/Ministry Grant)(Related to Political Justice & Weather) – Legacy & Property i.e. Forex
(In the form of Loan Credit Limit or Opportunity Reward) – from International Foundation Funds

Front Line Role & Marketing (Dominancy – 3th Rank)
(**Side Expenses**, Trading/Venture)(Related to Economic Conspiracy) – Option Trust i.e. Bonding
(In the form of Credit Rating or Influence Ergonomic) – from Regional Organisation Trade Deficit

From here, we can understand that Side Income from Ministry, Land Property or Intellectual Asset is far great important than a Back Stage Full Time Job. Apparently it proof the fitted postulated of Hybrid Job after a series of Plague.

Food and Drinks stand large portion. And most active is the Gold storage for War and Insurance Protection for Crime. Especially in current Economic Conspiracy and Celestial Conspiracy Era.

One to note that the Trade Deficit represent the influences or Authority of a Country or Organisation. It is either China or United States be the competition. By the way, it is important to have Public Image or Public Relations as Part time job, it stand very high portion toward Personal Finance.

Of course, the highest dominance comes from the Church Offering, and it count reversed to our tax cut at scale, and on turn we could have abundant of budget or allowance. For example, Church Fund those Heresy is very significant when come to Economics Conspiracy.

ii. The Introduction of New Economic System

Does Chinese Obey the Social Bonding? Since the Ancient Chinese, the Social Bonding start from Ancestry. That is general Germanic practised.

We have 3 group. Worship God, Worship Ancestry and Worship People. In which, Semitic Imperialism, Germanic Nationalism and African Popularism.

We have completing the defrag of 8 law out of 10 law from the hierarchy. Which is moderately high, called 猪八戒。

The more complete of defragment, the more complete of the Climate. Vice Verse. That how the Economic Crisis Happen, and predicting from 1997' to 2012' End time.

Social Disorder and Terrorism, Climate Change and Nuclear are on the same scenario. And the Virus Pandemic hold it all.

In another words, Virus Pandemic Census is crucial to gauge the Climate. vice versa. Got it? Weather good, Pandemic good. Pandemic Good Weather Good.

We cannot save Economic Crisis, but we can proceed Economic Crisis to next level. To avoid Ethnic Genocide is the Ultimate key thing to avoid Economic Crisis.

The Path is Start from Anti Semitic. Ok, let me more elaborate on Anti Semitic activities. It is the Light Code. Histogram. Classic, Mainstream, etc. The Cohedrant. Against this is Cult. 75% filled of Spirit. So if using benchmark in measure University Grade, School Result, is anti Semitic. Same thing to Currency and Electronic Currency.

Electronic Currency is to protect from Benchmark. No more inflation and Economic Crisis. I can say that. This New Economic Model taking the Individual Effort into Account. Money independent of time fade. The Credit or Loan Limit. That is Bitcoin, or NFT etc.

The Commonwealth Economic Model. Economic Activities yield Money. In compare to Financial Gain yield money. incl. Job Title you last. The Salary, Wage or Compesantion or Financial Gain called Population Ranking Money.

Depend on the Overall Benchmark. The Credit or Loan Limit is regardless of Benchmark but Evaluation. That is for example Land Property. And IPO and Market Launching is one of the way.

It is Universal or Directional? I advocate Directional. such as Bitcoin. The Bank play a crucial role. In precisely I called it Virtual Bank. As long as your effort is measured. The tangible value will be evaluated. Called it Sky Bank.

Again, money not by benchmark but by evaluation. I think its clear enough. The 7th Economic model is Brexit, thereafter Capitalism. In chinese, one mountain over one mountain. Unfair to have benchmark monetary system. Its a game of timing, i.e. Financial Game. Full Alert.

Conversely, its a game of information. No matter what, Electronic currency has adopt by Chinese. The advantage of Economic Premises. It is event oriented Monetary. The more worker involve the more harvest. The Federation. No Ecology System, No Mafia no Crime Oriented, No Colony Slave Oriented.

Communism 共产主义 (Career) 3 per – Population Dependent, Colony Slave Cult Crime. #5 **Financial Product Bidding** (Cash Interest/Tax). **GNP per capita**, UN (United States)

Federation 俄联邦 (Church) 7 per – Worker Population dependent & High Tech Mafia Oriented. #2 **Trade Deficit Sales Budget** (Financial Creditability Rating/Bitcoin). **National Productivity**, NATO (Russia)

Federalism 中央集权 (Family) 4 per – Ecosystem Economic, Mafia Crime Oriented. #3 **Centralised Commodity Funding** (Credit Limit/Debt). **GDP per capita**, WWF (China)

Nationalism 国民主义 (Nation) 8 per – Erotic Defect Economic Crisis Tendency, Nationalist War Crime Oriented. #4 **International Treaty** (Gold/Insurance). **Domestic Productivity**, KMT (Taiwan)

Capitalism 资本主义 (Marriage) 6 per – Economic Conspiracy, Terrorism Crime. #1 **Marketing Yield** (Fluid Asset Credential/Legacy). **GNI per capita**, NASA (Korea)

Commonwealth 英联邦 (Business) 5 per – Running Tax Business Owner, Organised Crime. #6 **Property Benchmark** (Fixed Asset/Intellectual Property). **National Income**, WHO (Japan)

iii. Colony Slave System

Let's Drop away Academic Excellency, and Promote toward Long Hierarchy Job for Good Social Orderliness. Japan and Singapore has good model on this.

Ban Colony & Slave System for immoral productivity gain. That is Communism Economic System, and current United States adopt.

President Lincoln Abolished Slave System. And Now United Nations Far East Countries bring it back.

Instead, a Healthy Economics as well as Working environment should be well bonded. Like what I advocated, Long Hierarchy Job Culture.

Short Hierarchy Job Culture, is Heavy Economic Loading. An Academic Excellency Job Culture is Social Disorder, for their skills set is about similar and very low standard deviation.

Long Hierarchy Job Culture that inclined toward Compensation as well asl Honour (Upstream), Time spent as well as Wage (Downstream), should be wide sought after, for a sustainable Booming Economy.

Racial Discrimination is expected but Gender Discrimination would be lesser. Let's create a better office and industry working environment and culture.

Happy Valentine Days!! May Good lovers be Good couples. Dare to be difference? Be the First Class. For that is Heavenly Love.

"Love is not about qualification so as Job. It's Organic Yoast."

D. Crime Disruption Highlights 犯罪捣破标记

Disclaimer: Independent Production, reinvent, disclosure, reproduction not granted.
承诺: 独立制作, 重译, 转载, 翻录必究。

- **Economic Conspiracy**
- **Economic Conspiracy with Capitalism**
- **Human Right Concerns**
- **Human Right Concerns Part II Nationalism**
- **Fund Analysis**
- **World Architecture related to proprietary history debate**
- **The 6 Perpetual Job, Biblical**

i. Economic Conspiracy

New World Order Conspiracy, e.g. Micron (Sub-level Chipset, populate Human Organ & Blood Trading) – Robotic Technology->Medicine Industry->Farmer (Acute Illness), Victim: Malaysia (Gen Z), Villain: Cult Syndicate Country (UN), United States & Australia

End of the World Conspiracy, e.g. Motorola a.k.a. Qualcomm (Sub-level Quantum Component, populate Satellite & Nuclear) – Applied Physics->Tourism industry->Detain & Prostitute (Human Right), Victim : Taiwan (Gen A), Villain: Low Tech Mafia Country (WWF), South America & Italy

Climate Change Conspiracy, e.g. UPS (Sub-level Courier, populate Ghost Account & Running Tax) – Logistic & Transportation Technology->Manufacturing Industry->White Collar (Chronic Illness), Victim : Singapore (Gen Y), Villain: Terrorism Country (NASA), Middle East & Korea Peninsular

World War Conspiracy, e.g. Dyson (Sub-level Motor, populate Rare Earth) – Quantum Technology->Mining Industry ->Soldier (Injury), Victim: Hongkong (Gen Q) & Organised Crime Country (WHO), Villain: United Kingdom & India

New Human Conspiracy, e.g. Barnes & Noble (Sub-level Copyright, populate Low Tax Credit) – Genetic Engineering->Drug Industry->Gangster (Jail), Victim: China (Gen W), Villain: High Tech Mafia Country (NATO), Europe & Russia

ii. Economic Conspiracy with Capitalism

1. Digital Economy – Blind Dog Machine (Anti Semitic)->New World Order (Obama & China)

2. End World Tourism – Erotic Flood (Anti Chinese)->Ethnic Genocide (Biden & Korea)

3. World War Rare Earth Quantum – Japan Intrusion (Anti Christ)->Chinese Poverty (Clinton & Singapore)

4. Climate Change Infrastructure Terrorism – Famine (Anti Jesus)->Plague (Bush & Taiwan)

5. Knowledge Economy Veterinary Medical – Popular Flu (Anti God)->AntiGod DNA modification (Trump & Japan)

iii. Human Right Concerns

1. Social Security/Accident or Injured Life Insurance *NATO* (Germany/Australia)

2. Hype Economic Culture/Cult activities or Erotic Defect *Vatican* (Italy/Netherland)

3. Psychology/Intellectual Credential *NASA* (Australia/Korea)

4. Psychiatry/War Criminal *FBI* (Japan/Hongkong)

5. Medicine/Epidemic Prevention or Ethical Treatment *WHO* (United Kingdom/France)

6. Fixed Property/Finance Credit Rating *WWF* (Russia/Turkey)

7. Marriage/Social Media Network or International Passport *UN* (China/Canada)

8. Job/Identity Card or Professional Status *KMT* (Taiwan/Malaysia)

9. Legitimate Business or Mafia/Credit Limit or Credit Card **CIA** (Singapore/Brazil)

10. Club membership/Privilege or Social Ranking **Zion** (United States/Israel)

The Leader is Vatican, Cult activities, Hype Economic Culture (Italy or Netherland)

iv. Human Right Concerns Part II Nationalism

1. **NATO** ally **Nazi Network (**Tionghua Chinese), All (Germany)
Social Security/Accident or Injured Life Insurance->**Disability**
Spy Agent/(Satan)士

2. **Vatican** ally **Taliban** (E-commerce Union a.k.a. Organ Trading Economy Conspiracy), False Spirit (Russia)
Hype Economic Culture/Cult activities or Erotic Defect->**Sudden Death**
Presidential Candidate/(Devil)將

3. **NASA** ally Paris Climate Change Treaty (**Diaspora Jew Union**), Psycho Science (Australia)
Psychology/Intellectual Credential->**Mental Rehab**
Astronaut/(Man of Sins)象

4. **FBI** ally Epoch, Aqueda Syndicate (**Last Samurai**), New Biblical Standard (Japan)
Psychiatry/War Criminal->**Chronic Drug**
Journalist/(False Prophet)車

5. **WHO** ally 007, Superman Syndicate (**Buckingha**m), Regenerative Medicine (United Kingdom)
Medicine/Epidemic Prevention or Ethical Treatment->**Hospitalised**
Doctor/(Dragons)馬

6. **WWF** ally Pizza Hut, Loser Syndicate (**Jewish**), Evil Spirit (Malaysia)
Fixed Property/Finance Credit Rating->**Bankruptcy**
Entrepreneur/(10 Kings of the World)馬

7. **UN** ally Holland, **Wife Syndicate** (Mexico), Old Biblical Standard (Korea)
Marriage/Social Media Network or International Passport->**Divorce**
Celebrity/(Repel Angel)帥

8. **KMT** ally Dagger Society, Casino Syndicate (**Imperial School**), Christian Mathematics (United States)
Job/Identity Card or Professional Status->**Murdering**
Lawyer/(False Christ or AntiChrist)士

9. **CIA** ally Twelve Lotus, Beggar Syndicate (**Qing Syndicate**), Christian Science (Singapore)
Legitimate Business or Mafia/Credit Limit or Credit Card->**Prison**
Soldier/(Serpent or Beast)相

10. **ZION** ally Shanghai Bund, **Joker Syndicate** (Dalai Lama), Pentecost Spirit (Taiwan)
Club membership/Privilege or Social Ranking->**Raping**
Mafia/(The Prostitute, Mafia)丰
The item (2) is the Lead.

v. Fund Analysis

A. Holding, Enterprise, Foundation (Intellectual Property)
Zero Trade Deficit, High Profit
Economic Crisis, **Fasci Economy Body**, Mafia Fund, Bond vs Fluid Asset
Buddhism, Federalism/Commonwealth, **WWF World Wide Reserved Fund**
Labour Union (Classical Music, Piano, Mode on Chord)
Anti Chinese/Anti Messiah (Family & Business Oriented)
Japan, United States Republican (Jew, Roman, French, Turkish), Romania, United
Kingdom & Singapore (Guangzhou, Suzhou, Zhejiang, Teochew)(PKR,PH)
Temasek Holding (Bad)

B. Equity, Organisation, Agency (Human Resource)
Largest Trade Deficit, Low Profit
Economic Booming, **Federation Economy Body**, Running Tax Fund, Gold vs
Insurance
Christianity, Federation Nationalism, **KMT Kuomintang**
Diaspora Jews Union (Blues Music, Guitar, Mode on Rhythm)
Anti Black/Anti God (Church & Nation Oriented)
North Korea, United States Military (Jude, Greek, Polish, Persian), Belarus, Russia &
Taiwan (Tangshan, Guangxi, Hainan, Guangdong)(PAS,MBF)
Fundsmith Equity (Good)

C. Investment Fund, Private Limited Company, Store (Land Property)
Low Trade Deficit, High Loss
Economic Conspiracy, **Nazi Economy Body**, Pentecostal Church Fund, Cash vs
Fixed Asset
Hinduism, Communism/Capitalism, **UN United Nations**
Chinese Union (Bossanova Music, Violin, Mode on Melody)
Anti Semitic/Anti Christ (Marriage & Job Oriented)
Korea, United States Democrat (Irish, Jewish, Germanic, Arabian), Ukraine,
Australia & Hongkong (Minnan, Fujian, Guangfu, Fuzhou)(UMNO,DAP)
Vanguard LifeStrategy 80% Equity/GIC Singapore (Good and Bad)

From above Structure Data, we may know the where major Funding of Covid-19 as
well as where the Backing Funding.

- The GIC Singapore Investment Funding is to support the **Marketing Budget**.
- The Marketing Budget is to spread over the **Covid-19 Fake News**.
- The World Wide **News Broadcast** Location is the Location full of Events.
- It must be in **Geneva Time -8.30hr**, and Singapore is among Asia Four Dragons fit the bill.
- The Israel time the best **Geneva Time -1hr**.
- **Ukraine** is in the list.
- However, the **Highest Suspicious Funding is Korea**, the World Wide News Broadcast Location. a.k.a. **Cult Fund**.

- i.e. **United Nations Funding**.
- The **Backing Fund** is the Funding backing the Marketing Budget.
- It must be a Precious & Established **Land Property**.
- It is a place full of **Bankruptcy** due to Casino, Mafia, Porn, and College.
- Temasek Holding Geographical Location is **Kuala Lumpur. a.k.a. Mafia Fund.**
- All of this called **Nazi Economy Body.**
- This is to **excluding Qing Syndicate** function such as Running Tax.
- It is important to evaluate the cause effect to find out the **Disruption Path.**
- i.e. **Cult Fund vs Mafia Fund**
- **GIC (United Nation Fund) and Temasek (Federalism Mafia Fund) are the World Most Active Fund.**
- **Seoul vs Shanghai** or **Perth vs Kuala Lumpur**, or **Ukraine vs France**
- The most active Place is **Perth vs Kuala Lumpur.**
- This explain the Covid-19 Research Lab and **Nazi Headquarter.**

vi. World Architecture related to proprietary history debate

1. Military Network, 6D Whiteboard, NATO (Germany)(Illustration)
Mariology Theology a.k.a. Marriage Law i.e. Christian Law

Figure 20 Germany Castle

2. Political Network, 10D Herald, (Event Classify), Vatican (Russia)(Prophecy)
The Insect-Borned Virus 2016' in Amazon River is a masterpiece of a Mafia. It remains a direct link to Covid-19 as there are closed Protein.

Figure 21 Russia Novodevichy Conveent

3. Genius Network, 3D ISBN, (Geographical Classify), NASA (Australia)(Philosophy)
Copyright War United States versus China. The Corruption and Fall of Eastern Orthodox or Protestant Church. The Christian Science (Gospel) Approach versus Christian Mathematic (Revelation) Approach and Christian Arts (Old Testament).

shutterstock.com · 102344032

Figure 22 Australia Sydney Theatre

4. Conspiracy Network, 8D Bulletin, FBI (Japan)(Clues)

The China '64' rootcause fall within Japan or Germany. The Disruption of Fasci or Nazi.

Figure 23 Japan Tokyo Tower

5. Elderly Network, 7D Journal (Ethnic Classify), WHO (United Kingdom)(Concept)

Imperial Law Implementation as well as Nutriology to Public Health.

Figure 24 United Kingdom London Bridge

6. Entrepreneurship Network, 4D Whitepaper (Career Classify), WWF (Malaysia)(Content)

Digital Economy Conspiracy Disruption. Clean Energy and Electric Car. The Risen or Fall of Tycoons or Giants.

Figure 25 Malaysia Petronas Twin Tower

7. Marriage Network, 1D Telegram, (Age Classify), UN (Korea)(Alarm)

Economic War United States versus China, in lier of Rocket Science Economy to Vietnam Cold War to Pacific World War.

Figure 26 Korea Monument

8. Religion Network, 4D Broadcast, (Politics Classify), KMT (United States)(Body Language)

Political Revolution Review in terms of Taiwan Independency Military Endervour, Chauvinism

1800′(文革初期,小刀会又名上海滩)–Joshua001:叶问 (Hongkong)(Imperialism)

1915′(五四运动,鲁迅)–Joshua002:孙中山 (Taiwan)(Nationalism)

1966′(文化大革命,金庸,琼瑶)–Joshua003:李小龙 (Singapore)(Popularism)

2010′(六四经济开放,Beyond)–Joshua004:成龙 (Malaysia)(Chauvinism)

A Turkish Match to Religion Unity.

Figure 27 United States Iconic Landmark

9. News Network, 9D Channel, (Wealth Classify), CIA (Singapore)(Radio)

'911' '311' & Covid-19 Rootcause and thoroughly Disruption of Ethnic Genocide.

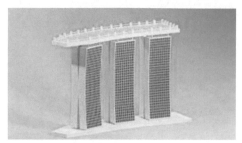

Figure 28 Singapore the Sand Casino Tower

10. Labour Network, 2D Forum, ZION (Taiwan)(Message)

National Security Law victim are Club Member versus Porn Member.

Figure 29 Taiwan Taipei 101 Tower

vii. The 6 Perpetual Job, Biblical

Each Character cope with combinative of Jobs (Backstage and Frontstage)(Major and Minor).

Technical
A1. James, Programmer->Engineer
A2. Moses, Chef->Scientist
A3. Santa, Architect->Inventor

Accounting
B1. Jehovah, Governor->Tax collector
B2. Joseph, Landlord->King
B3. Jacob, Slave->Banker

Marketing
C1. Mary, Servant->Queen
C2. Nehemiah, Clerk->Prostitute
C3. Eve, Manager, Dictator

Sales
D1. Jesus, Entrepreneur
D2. Joshua, Trader
D3. David, Business Owner

Financial
E1. Christ, Investor
E2. Solomon, Author
E3. Adam, Soldier

Personnel
F1. Messiah, Celebrity
F2. Esther, Journalist
F3. Lawrence, Doctor

E. War Highlights 战争标记

Disclaimer: Independent Production, reinvent, disclosure, reproduction not granted.
承诺: 独立制作, 重译, 转载, 翻录必究。

- **World War is Final**
- **如何对抗纳粹与联合国。**
- **Let's called the things off.**
- **The 2nd Home of Nazi**
- **Headquarter of Nazi Economy Body**
- **Terrorism Funding & 1Malaysia Development Berhad i.e. 1MDB**
- **Salvation to Chinese**

i. World War is Final

Guarantor. Let's share.. This is the secret to defeat your opponent. The Brake. A Machine cannot without Stopper, Brake or Escape, Reset.

A Syndicate cannot stand without Sign board. An Economy Body cannot survive without Command. i.e. Instruction not Manual. The Picture, for real human. Economy Body required Real Human. Thats How Nazi growth.

Communist against and dislike Nazi. UN is not equal to Nazi. World War sought after than Cold War. Cold war is not final.

Ultimate Crime Disruption is toward Economy Body. e.g. Knowledge Economy is Medicine. Without Indicator, economy cannot sustain. That the job we need to eliminate to Nazi.

ii. 如何对抗纳粹与联合国。

A picture meant a thousand words. 是我们的朋友，是我们的敌人？Keep your ass shut. 今天的主题是要探讨灵恩派的逆向教导。对不起，在这之前，我想要对纳粹做个总结。这对 Covid-19 病变破解非常关键。反对声量越大，身为使徒的我们越要坚持。尽管今天的工作是我独自一人。身为盐的我们，独自一人力量可以是强大千万 Lumen，即是 Supernova。

废话不多说。言归正传，基督教会可分为九份。就是一正，一邪。路德宗新教，加尔文派，长老会很有名望，被误判为邪派。顺势起兵的是灵恩派的崛起。被看成反德国路德宗。这两派的斗争是纳粹与联合国之争。纳粹法西斯制度是制造经济体与基督对抗。反基督主义。而那经济体就是各纳粹成员。当然赔本生意。无法赚正当钱财。如恐怖主义金融危机引发气候变化，疫情病毒疫苗欺骗，核武地产泡沫等

所以说，做坏事不能挣钱。让我们看看西方国家的经济。纳粹成员在亚洲。西方的经济非常健全，识字率很高。所以西方的高等教育是全面开放的，不会供不应求。这就是经济发达。看看东方国家，识字率不在话下，知识分子被文字狱。等等。我们中国人抬不起头是因为没钱。我的天。

所以打击纳粹经济体的方法就是玩金钱游戏。就是发动世界大战。在六大经济体的博弈中，最终胜出的必定是俄联邦为首。胜券在握。都说了，做坏事挣不了钱的。收旧报纸吧。

这信用额度越来越儿戏。鬼才信你。没错，华尔街股盘。无法交出成绩单。铤而走险。是偏向联合国这边。共产党经济。林肯废除的奴隶制度又回来了。在这样的体制下，世界大战稳亏的。是时候把一条腿从亚洲撤退。东方的时代还没到。修复以色列城墙是当下之急。

看看中国各大城市与新加坡的摩登化？几乎就是开倒车。改革开放中国就是六四！！对与错我们交给历史裁判。吃苹果太多，变成'恰恰'！！红海行动是必须的。始终贯一。习主席辛苦了。中美合一是当下局势。

现在开始进入灵恩派的逆向教导课题。基督教导可分为现实，末世，天国。逆向教导有，摩西十诫，末世盼望，天国爱情。就是信，望，爱。

摩西十诫的亲和力，反之为猪八戒。举例，崇拜不可知伪善力量；惯性迫切祷告；金钱孝道，等等。

曲解之下末世盼望变成，无花果长叶子是坏人觉醒；东方闪电与秃鹰是恐怖主义；假基督与假基督徒是灵恩派；救世主与海啸是疫情肆虐等。打击邪恶势力的盼望扭曲成经济阴谋。

天国爱情，地下捆绑的，天上也捆绑。天上释放，地上也释放。天国爱情就是地球的爱情，一样的。爱情是现实不是理想。错，天国不娶也不嫁。自由恋爱，柏拉图爱情。足以构成了成千上万的爱情故事。

这就是灵恩派的逆向教导带来的狂热。就是无神论，拜金主义！！

– 全文完 –

iii. Let's called the things off.

The War Treaty
The initiative of Russia control the Corner of Europe continent is apparently valid, that due to current World Office is dominated in the Wrong hands.

War Crime
Nazi Economic Body members performs, 1. Economics Conspiracy by Clean Energy for World War. 2. Epidemic by Knowledge Economy Corruption i.e. Medicine Industry 3. Erotic Defect & Genocide, Social Disorder & New World Order by Anti Semitic 4. Economic Crisis for Control Weather.
These Big Four Major War Crime.

Schism to United States
Due to these, I have reasons to vote a better World Government or Create Schism in United States the Big Brother. We have to endervour to avoid War, if it is extra works.

Marxism Ideology the Communism Ideology
Of course the Schism in United States is not about Germanic or African Human Right but Semitic Human Right. This is the Justice, for Law practise some many years thru the formed of Israel, in 5000 years. Those under suffering and tortured are those Semitic, even still now. Human Right on African is about Religious Movement. and surprisingly, Colony and Slave system is wide accepted in African Community. Which is so called White Collar Wild Fire. This Marxism Ideology called Communism Ideology. Feed those needy. In fact most of the time is exchange with Pride and Erotic.

Communism and Religious Activities to World Village
For this Religious Movement transform into United Nations, guarding the Democracy Wild Fire Globally. And the so called Democracy in fact Communism Nazi Economic Body. Oriental Democracy is False Democracy. The What the Schism of United States would yield from. I know alot of Jew pivot their land to New Zealand and Australia. Let's face the reality, we are to be Colonised. No matter what, this is the awakening calls and not suppose drop into War Banner. But to disrupt Communism and so called Religious Activities we need Economic Booming and Medicine Renaissance. And fully equip to face the No Justice. After all, Background will change, but Election will not changed.

Say Yes to Real Heaven
World Village i.e. Utopia is for those Undergraduate. Say yes to Real Heaven. All are precious.

Say No to War

Romance of three kingdom. Let's justice prevail. When talk is not useful, we need self defences. War is for Pride at Price. There is No loser in a War, but Victim. I suggest Summit talk if there is no allergy. Those allergy not fit. We need pay money for eyes those enemy, not to pay eye for eye. This would be Genius. Lets God power heal the Kingdom. We are in a Solar System of all connected, one branch fail, all can feel. All branch need well positioning, called Hierarchy.

Prevail those Outside when End Time
Let recognise what Authentic and what Official. Christianity will prevail outside the Church when end time. Mathematically. Professionals will prevail outside the Office when end time. Mathematically either.
When you see these sign, the enemy has arrive, so as Ally. For those Official is Opposite. Don't be faith off but keeping the long road. There are alot of judge in Islam. As Christian don't be judger, but Observer. And pass the Message to next 14 generations. History will not prevail but Story will prevail.

The After Life the Eternal life
That is what we endervour, Spiritual Miracle thru all stories. and formed up Principle and then to Law. The Systematic 10 law hierarchy. Law of Moses, the Semitic Law. Those who are belong to Evil, you will not hurt. But those Righteous would face, age, sick and dead. The Spirit Prevail outside the Official Body. After Life, the Eternal Life when end time. Those Evil will continue enjoy in Earth Village so called Utopia for so called Plato Love. That called Immortal.

Let's called the things off.

iv. Headquarter of Nazi Economy Body

Today the Ukraine crisis is the War on the cause of False Democracy. It is in fact the Capitalism game. Let's shut the door of Economic Conspiracy but welcome Economic Ministry. That is what we need.

The Federalism Economic i.e. Fasci Japan doing that promote the Economic Conspiracy by side. And the Japan Mafia Funding is centred on Chinese. Let's make peace of China and Japan diplomacy. That what Chinese Leader ought to concern.

What if the life had a 2nd Chance? What if for a Regime?

By the way, to make correction. There is one United States, formed by Democrat, Republican and Federalism. Not 1 in 3 but 3 in 1. United Nations stay away from United States and that is Oriental Democracy a.k.a. Communism.

All country shall one day aligned in the Meta Universe.

Democracy correspond to War Syndicate; Republican correspond to Organised Syndicate; and Federalism correspond to Mafia. Australia-Taiwan-Korea; United Kingdom-Hongkong-Japan; France-Singapore-North Korea.

All of these called United Nations, Communism Cult Syndicate. Germany-Malaysia-China Malaysia and China is rule out.

And Germany is truly the so called "Oriental Democracy", Communism and Headquarter of Nazi Economy Body.

If we can address this, we can avoid deep into war. Make your voice.

Economy Demography

United Kingdom & Denmark-Singapore-Japan; **Australia (Brisbane) & United States Monarchy i.e. Whitehouse**-Commonwealth (Semitic & Anglo)-Qing Syndicate a.k.a. WHO, (PKR,PH -practitioner, white collar, hygienic first) **Running Tax-Economic Booming** (Tourism Point)(Multimedia Corridor) 火

Russia & Austria-Taiwan-Korea; **Australia (Melbourne) & United States Democracy i.e. Pentagon**-Capitalism-Federation (Jude & Irish)-Nationalism a.k.a. KMT, (PAS,BN -technician, blue collar, safety first) **War-Economic Recession** (Infrastructure Estate)(Iskandar Industrial Park) 雷

France & Italy-Malaysia-North Korea; **Australia (Adelaide) & United States Republican**-Federalism (Jew & British)-Fasci Japan a.k.a. WWF, (PN,MCA -researcher, green collar, pollution first) **Mafia-Economic Crisis** (Education Hub)(Singapore Malaysia Rail Way) 水

Germany & Netherland-Hongkong-China; **Australia (Sydney) & United States**
Royalism i.e. Oriental Democracy-Communism (Jewish & Scottish)-Nazi Germany
a.k.a. UN (UMNO,DAP -administrator, pink collar, ethic first)
Cult-Economic Conspiracy (Financial Centre)(Proton) 风

v. The 2nd Home of Nazi

Church Reformation
We need stay on the top as Righteous. Not follow the norms, and become illness and compromise security. To do that, we need reform our Music. The Church Music. There is a typical. and Good Song and Bad Song is micron distance.

Pillar of all Music
The African Jazz. Very Classic. But I tell you it is the Pillar of all music. Same thing to Hymn music, and Rock all three Pillar. The Median are those Dance Music. All Similarity. The Jazz or Hymn or Rock either one is Evil. This is come from Formation of 9 algorithm. Heaven Music, Paradise Music and Earthly Music.

Differ in Metric Scale i.e. Musical Scale
There all are same algorithm but different Scale. The difference here, 88 Progressive weighted Keys and 66 time sensitive keys or 77 weighted Keys The Hymn is evil. Electronic Midi Music, Wire Plugged Mp3 Music and Acoustic DVD 24K Music. I beat off. Rock not yet expanding, Hymn can be expanding, but Jazz has already expanded. The Original is Rock. The Highest Rank. Jazz is evil music.

Music Economy
Copy Cat. No offend. Rock and Roll is the Original Music. Jazz is derivative works. Score reading same as Classical Song. Name famous Rock Artist, Elton John, Beatles, Elvis Presley. Fundamentalist Winner, Episcopal 2nd, then Pentecostal. Of course, we cannot force people to listen our music. That why Rock Album is Free. Jazz Music most expensive due to Marketing Scheme.This called Music Economy.

Three type of Church Music
Rock Artist earn advertisement contract. How to write a Rock Song? We know Hymn song is interpolated Writing. Jazz is Running Bass Writing.Rock is Progression of Chord Circle of Firth Writing. Jazz is expensive and Luxury. Rock is concert recording. The layout of Church Music should reform as Self Praise Song, Poetry Song, and Worship Song The prayer is as follow, Self Praise Song is Miracle, Poetry Song is Healing, Worship Song is Salvation. Junk song are those mixed these 3. And become Trinity Song, White Song and Trinity Church is White Church. For Jesus is not Music, God is Light. Jesus is not Church, God is Nation.

The Land the Music
For those Obey Semitic Law, they can enjoy the Promised Land.The New Canaan Economic Abundancy. For those Obey Roman Law, they can enjoy Freedom. For those Obey Moses Law, they can enjoy Miracle of Heaven. Let know the major differ, Roman is Cult Blind Follow, Semitic is Mafia Thief, Arabian is Non Social Bonding Marriage Disorder.

Geography and Politics

Conversely, Roman Land is West Span to East. Land of Full of Opportunities. Lucky land. Where Scientific Discovery build on But Lonely Road. Know why? There are Ethnic Line, Information Line, Research Line, and Virus Line. And Ukraine is the Ethnic Line of Europe. This is the Culture City. Cultural dominated City. There are Black Sea. Aegen sea. What culture Russia could bring in? Human Right Culture True Human Right Culture. Same to Bible and Differ from Martin Luther King Junior.

Human Right and Politics

In Europe alot of Jew Jude Irish Anglo Semitic suffer Anti Semitic Popularism. To Rule the Land of Ukraine, rule the Human Right of Europe. Same time abolish, Gender equality, Same Sex Marriage, Equal Wage, Mental Health Discrimination, Politics, and Mafia. The High Tech Mafia instead. Church is First Priority. Its right time to review Human Right, its human past life, present life, future life, after life and eternal life. All voices all letter all complaint shall get addressed. This is true human right. Voice comes first.

Humanity and War

Its time to review what our humanity after World War II dominated by former Nazi and Present UN. The communism economy body. The cruel war crime of Myanmar, Vietnam, China Tiananmen 64, Hongkong Extradition Law, Taiwan Civil War, Korea Civil War. Its about Fundamentalist, Episcopal and Pentecostal Wrestling. Which is the Hinduism, Buddhism and Islam wrestling. Add one more, Xinjiang Education Camp.

Economics and Humanity

In fact the tortured rehab and prison. We come to a point conclude the Force of Economic Power was from Asia.as Equity index is very high for Communism Country. They opt out US Stock. And inclined to non semitic stock. This is how communism Economic Body moves. Bank Merger, Company Merger, Colony Slave working Culture. To increase the Benchmark Score in Financially. We shall parallel disrupt the Headquarter of Nazi and Stop Abuse Military as well as War Crime to Civilian. This is a dead end, we have to be responsible. Confess the wrong, and recognised what you raised. This is Non Limited Royal Flush readiness. Fold at any circumstance of repent. No kids.

Repent and make Change

and after all its to switch From UN to Vatican sovereign. Nazi to Fasci. Its WWF. Reserved the Culture and Land. African is culprit of Communism as well as Arabian. The FIFA 2022. Ukraine is innocent, please spare their life, but sign war treaty. We need to vote a New World Government to replace the Colony Slave Minded WHO and UN. Lincoln Abolished Slave System, I abolished Oriental Human Right. Yes I abolished Oriental Human Right, will not vote Communist and Arabian.

Choose Treaty avoid War

Called One man dream. When come to War Treaty and War, I choose Treaty and No war. No War called Cold War in fact. Yes its strategy location required self guard and patience. The Ukraine. Rule the Land, Rule the Law. Invasion like Mongolia styled. War crime is not worthy. Please think twice. Justice is hiding, don't test it. Never test justice, you will cheer off. But we can test Friendship by denied. Organic 3 times is meant gone. There is no real friendship, all are benefit exchange. Enemy can be Ally, Ally can be enemy. If you change your orientation. To Crime Disruption, this is over-committed. To Human Right of All man kind this is justified. For Human Right is simple a Protest. But Crime Disruption you require alot of Social Science combine with Science forensic. This is a Wrong Move. Germany has moved. For Berlin Wall, it is become Fundamentalist Church country. Christian Devout Country.

Asia the 2nd Home of Nazi

But look at the Economic of Asia, we need Russia assist. Ukraine Conquer is truly wisdom but this not cheap. We have to pay the price if victory. All Unit Standby. Keep off distance, we required ally. Say hi to Islam. Turkey in the straw. Together we are strong. But you are not my friend. This is beneficial exchange only. This is life, and war. Same. Man switch fast, this is Quran. Stop Machi, No Friendship such thing, but Hero Egoism. If you think this is beneficial we can work together, how career like that. No relationship. For Relationship is on Marriage and Family. 5000 years. Diplomacy is yes. No terrorism. No Utopia Build own dream. Heaven is true for all religion.

So the Sky. Reach the sky, reach the heaven.

vi. Terrorism Funding & 1Malaysia Development Berhad i.e. 1MDB

Let's break down the cause and effect.

- Previous analysis, Kuala Lumpur Malaysia is right to be called Mafia Headquarter.
- This rule out Malaysia is not Terrorism Hiding Place.
- The 1MDB Funding is in turn belong to Organised Crime Syndicate.
- And the 1MDB Funding is a False case.
- Terrorism Funding is Federation Economic Body.
- Beside Russia, Singapore is one of the Federation Economic Body in which they promote Economic Booming.
- And very high GNP per Capita index i.e. Health Index.

vii. Salvation to Chinese

Racial Riot a.k.a. Ethnic War (Wrestling about Commodities)
WWI Mafia Syndicate War, Roman vs Anglo
West Europe Mafia (a.k.a. Italy Mafia) vs East Europe Mafia (a.k.a. East India Company)

Civil War a.k.a. Religion War (Wrestling about Financial Credit Rating)
WWII Organised Syndicate War, Eastern Orthodox vs Catholic
Russian Organised Syndicate (a.k.a. Russia Bratva) vs Singapore Organised Syndicate (a.k.a. Qing Syndicate)

World/Cold War a.k.a. Technology/Economic War (Wrestling about Intellectual Property)
WWIII Cult Syndicate War, Traditional Atheism vs Charismatic Wave
Asia Cult Syndicate (a.k.a. Fasci Japan) vs Western Cult Syndicate (a.k.a. Nazi Germany)

Mafia and Organised has to be allied. Let's draw your and our boundary.

Possess the Rocket Science and Earth Science knowledge is a must in World War Era. Leveraging, and equip yourself. Of course before that you need to join Church.

Christianity can be a long journey. Calvinism Theology is biased to Western. We need equip with Spirit and Wisdom.

Failed to do, you have to catch up. Time's urs.

In salvation its benchmark instead of evaluation. Opps.

F. Religion Highlights 宗教标记

- **Oriental Blueprint**
- **Oriental Judgement**
- **End time Villains**
- **Oriental Judgement Part II**
- **The Equipping of Authentic Christian**
- **Four Image of God**
- **Silk Road 40 Years Transition from Israel Wall 500 years**

i. Oriental Blueprint

Promised Land, A.D. 1'-Present (Asia Four Small Dragon i.e. Four Economic Premises of Chinese)

1. **Commonwealth**: Buddhism, Chinese->**Singapore**, SME (End loop, Resurrection), Pseudo Science, Electrical Machine, Organised Crime, Digital Conspiracy, Living Organ Trading, Agriculture Economy, Anti-Semitic (NATO)

2. **Capitalism**: Christianity, Germanics->**Taiwan**, F&B (Free Loop, Empire Age I,II,III), Economic Science, Telecommunication, Terrorism, Climate Change Conspiracy, Mental Abduction, Infrastructure Economy, Anti-Christ (NASA)

3. **Federalism**: Islam, African->**Hongkong**, Public (Big Loop, World War I,II,III), Applied Physics, Mechanical Transportation, Mafia, Medical Conspiracy, Virus Outbreak, Knowledge Economy, Anti-God (WWF)

4. **Communism**: Heresy, Semitic->**Korea**, MNC (Small Loop, Economic Crisis I,II,III), Genetic Science, Ergonomic, War Crime, End World Conspiracy, Erotic Defect, Tourism Economy, Anti-Chinese (United Nations)

Promised Land to Eden Garden, to Oriental (Jerusalem Wall from Christianity to Islam)(Silk Road from Buddhism to Hinduism)

1. Cold War villain->United Nations (New Babylon, Islam), Korea (Nuclear), Russia (Erotic Defect), victim (Germanic)

2. Racial Riot villain->NATO (Promised Land, Buddhism), United Kingdom (Terrorism), Singapore (Living Organ Trading), victim (African)

3. World War villain->NASA (Oriental, Hinduism), Taiwan (Tsunami), Australia (Mental Abduction), victim (Chinese)

4. Civil War villain->WWF (Eden Garden, Christianity), Hongkong (Virus), United States (Virus Outbreak), victim (Semitic)

Loop Diagram of Selection of Oriental (Span of 1000 years)

1. End Loop, Cold War, Resurrection I,II (~500 years), Judgement->Oriental I,II (Cult Place, Olive Tree Place)->New Jerusalem I,II (Living Organ Trading to African) e.g. Semitic, Egyptian

2. Free Loop, Racial Riot, Empire Age I,II,III (~150 years), Technology/Religion Revolution->Theology Foundation, I,II,III Calvinism (ergonomic),Arminianism (placebo),Anabaptism (spiritual)->New Medicine I,II,III (Virus to Semitic) e.g. Ergonomic Genetic Science->Physiology Drug Science->Psycology Psycho Science

3. Big Loop, World War I,II,III, (~40 years), Civilisation/Ethnicity Revolution->Liberal Land a.k.a. New Canaan I,II,III (Erotic Defect to Germanic)(Europe, Russia, United States)->Technology Breakthrough e.g. Pseudo Science a.k.a. Christian Mathematics (Biblical Science), Applied Physics a.k.a. Christian Arts (Pentecost Science), Economic Science a.k.a. Christian Science (Quantum Science)

4. Small Loop,Economic Crisis I,II,III (~10 years), Economics/Politics Evolution->Economics Protocol I,II,III (Quaratine to Chinese)(Joshua for Elders>James for Youth>Santa for Children)->New Climate Change Treaty I,II,III e.g. Theoretical, Practical, Literal

ii. End time Villains

1. **Rebel Angels**->Cult Church (Epidemic & Plague)(Korea), UN

2. **Chinese Dragons**->Qing Syndicate (Conspiracy & Terrorism)(Japan), NATO

3. **False Christ**->Zion Organisation (Economic Crisis & Nuclear)(China), WWF

4. **The Prostitute, Mafia**->Nazi Syndicate (Crime Disorder & Jail Terrorism)(United States), KMT

5. **Devil/Satan, Beast/Serpent,False Prophet/Man of Sins**->Joker Syndicate (Abduction/Dishonouring & Social Disorder, Poverty, Global Warming)(Australia), NASA

6. **10 Kings of the World**->Forbes Top 10 & Royals (Erotic Defect & Genocide)(United Kingdom), WHO

A. Cold War->Epidemic & Plague->Rebel Angels->Perfect Christian->**Moon Jae-in**?->**The Highest Fluid Asset Country (Highest GNI per capita)->Moon Jae-in (Confirmed)**

B. Civil War->Economic Crisis & Nuclear->False Christ

C. World War->Global Warming & Terrorism->i. **Man of Sins**>ii. **Satan** >iii. **Devil & Beast, False Prophet**

iii. The Equipping of Authentic Christian

Safety Net to Parachute
Just one more time. Ground is non necessary. But Pillar. We all have to learned. 2 colour wires. There automatic cut-off resistor. At light speed. Kindergarten is extra, Primary is for fun. Fundamental and Ultimate is what we seeking. Paper flight. This is blur you off to read the musical note. The variety of Programming Language. The Variety of drawing suite. Mathematics Algebra Analysis. By using 9 page of paper we can have calculate the typical Enzyme for Corona Virus. Bullshit… Human create non equal, some can read musical note, some cannot. some can read algebra analysis, some cannot. some can read 2D or 3D drawing, some cannot. some can read statistic chard, some cannot. some can read military diagram, some cannot. some can read chemistry bonding, some cannot.

Authentic versus Official
The reason here, because of gifted. If you are not gifted, you have to learn fundamental to equip. Of course you are working isolation. This is the different of Microsoft and Macintosh. Work out from office. Walk out from Church. Walk out from School. Those are God raised. Heaven is belong to Champion. Separate righteous from normal. Qualification is formatted. The Official. Experience is Organic. The Authentic.

The Risen of Worthy
Do your best. Its recommended for all, life is a war, life is a gamble. You want security, you self lock. Freedom is organic. The life. Some land has life, some land doesn't has life. Calvary hill. Highest prestige ranking of life. One die save all. This is called Land. the particular land. With perfect order of Law, it become miracles. Where else? Don't believe you eye but gut. There is no land holy than Mt Sinai. Holy land vanished begin from end time.

Sin free versus Holy
This is Climate Change. The conjugate is quantum wave. Nuclear weapon cause Climate Change. Nuclear Power Plant cause Climate Change. Its have to be double action. And that is Holy Saint privilege. Holy Saint. Righteous is not holy. God want us peace. Jesus wants us victory. Freedom from sins. Is not always freedom from crime. But it expanded and derivative from crime. Crime yield sins. There are no Perfect Crime. No one. But the one virgin conceived. We all are non holy, but free from sins. Once again, free from sins is confession and buy your shit or gift. To be sin free. What you pursuit for? Sin free or Holy?

Righteous i.e. Sin Free
Righteous is the explanation of Sin free. How to be righteous? Its risk management strategy you have to overcome. Its the grace of people. They are selectively. Righteous is simply a letter or words.To present to your enemy. Its not judgemental. The way you treat your enemy, called righteous. It about something or condition, not kids toy. Righteous women most the time are love story. Fictional.

Differ in Man and Women

Holiness women is history. There non righteous women in history. if yes that is fictional. Women are precious. They cannot imagine Jesus is man. Fully man Fully God. They always imagine Jesus is almighty can do. No greater. All are automatic granted. Jesus in fact always lose. This due to Jesus is fully man. Believed Jesus are weak are righteous. Believed Jesus is strong are those literates.
Raise Righteous

The Bible in Science terms

Those lucky are those holiness. Those Happiness are those Righteous. Those Health are those hold Justice. Those in war are those in Love. This is Laplace Christian Science Circle of Fifth No mention. If there is war, there is love. Give and take. There is healthy, there is Justice. There is Criminal, there is bad luck. There is secular, there is prostitute. There is rich, there is prostitute. Those Poverty is happiness. Make clear, Gospel using Christian Science and Applied Physics and Medicine Science together. Christiaan just part of it. Game Theory, Quantum Computing and Laplace Transform. All constitute Gospel. And that is Holistic, localised. Require 4 binder. One world Four system. To them is World War. To us is Cold War. Act and Epistle is about homogenous. That is Pentecost era. End time. 1000 years cycle. Homogenous is individual. What you see is not what I see. That is the definition of love specially tailor for you. 1 Corinthians 13:48. Each one of us has ours. All different meaning tailor individual. The Revelation number. This is avatar. The Old Testament is schematic diagram. Its Arts. The Law is an arts. Its spatial. 3D i.e. 360Deg x 360Deg. Once Law justified, it become reality.

What all about Bible least, is Human Right

Human Right Acts is not justifiable Law. Virtual. That the reason Taiwan failed. To enforce Human Right Acts is to make it become into Treaty. Using the imperialism method to operate the Human Right Acts. There isnt Human Right Law in Bible, but Quran. To implement, required enforcement. or it is just a plain guideline for hobbies.

iv. Oriental Judgement

1. **World Threats**: Economic Conspiracy Disruption *(Capitalism to Evil)* ->End time Villain Judgement (UN Chairman)

2. Civilisation & Humanity a.k.a. **World Issue** *(Erotic Defect & Ethical error)*: World War and Cold War readiness->Semitic 12sects Judgement (Crime Syndicate)

3. **Climate Change** Root Cause *(Anti Semitic to Social Disorder)*: Economic Crisis->False Christ Judgement (The most Righteous Person)

4. **Religion Unity** *(Anti Chinese & Ethnic Supremacy)*: Silk Road 40 Years Transition from Israel Wall 500 year->Repentance of Qing Syndicate (Manchu)

5. **Salvation** of Gentile *(Practical to Secular)*: Speed Evangelism->Forbidden Fruit or Skip Baptism Judgement (Forbidden Fruit to Evil minded)

6. **Spiritual War** *(Heresy or Cult)*: Speed Reformation->Dark Magic or White Magic Judgement (most Dark Magic)

7. **Victory Closure** *(Heavy Burden)*: New Medicine->The Separation from Righteous (Devoted Person)

v. Oriental Judgement Part II

Theology (Spiritual Body): Eastern Orthodox (Christianity, Multi-theism), **NATO/FBI Federation** (Cybercrime, Church)
Blues (88 Key Progressive Weighted), Matrices (Multiple Rhythm)
7per Hexagram, Revelation, Chemical, Heaven, 6G, World War (Erotic Defect), Span 100 years
Heaven: New Judah ->Jude (Hongkong)
Clean Energy Economy – World War Conspiracy

Psycho Science (Holy Spirit): Fundamentalism (Islam, Trinity), **KMT/WHO Nationalism** (War, Nation)
Rock (88 Key Weighted), Game Theory (Progression Chord)
6per Pentecost, Epistle, Electronics, Oriental, 5G, Cold War (Human Organ Trading), Span 500 years
Oriental: New Canaan ->Jew (Taiwan)
Digital Economy – New World Order Conspiracy

Medicine (Body & Soul): Episcopal (Buddhism, Atheism), **WWF/Vatican Federalism** (Mafia, Family)
Hymn (77 Key Semi Weighted), Fourier Series (Expanding Melody)
5per Quantum, Gospel, Electrical, Paradise, 4G, Civil War (Economic Crisis), Span 5 years
Promised Land: New Bethlehem->Semitic (Singapore)
Infrastructure Economy – Climate Change Conspiracy

Genetics (Body): Pentecostal (Hinduism, Monotheism), **NASA/UN Capitalism** (Terrorism, Marriage)
Jazz (66 Key Time Sensitive), Laplace Transform (Running Bass)
4per Biblical, Old Testament, Mechanical, Hell, 3G, Racial Riot (Genocide), Span 50 years
Utopia: New Jerusalem ->Levi (Korea)
Knowledge Economy – New Human Conspiracy

vi. Four Image of God

Spiritual Body: Eastern Orthodox (Christianity, Multi-theism)
Revelation, Heaven
Clean Energy Economy e.g. Tesla – World War Conspiracy
St Joseph vs Satan

Holy Spirit: Fundamentalism (Islam, Trinity)
Epistle, Oriental
Digital Economy e.g. Google – New World Order Conspiracy
Transformer vs False Prophet

Body & Soul: Episcopal (Buddhism, Atheism)
Gospel, Promised Land
Infrastructure Economy e.g. Samsung – Climate Change Conspiracy
Seagull vs False Christ

Body: Pentecostal (Hinduism, Monotheism)
Old Testament, Utopia
Knowledge Economy e.g. Amazon – New Human Conspiracy
Jehovah vs Devil

vii. Silk Road 40 Years Transition from Israel Wall 500 years.

2G to 3G Berlin Wall, Israel Wall and China Great Wall (World War Era 5000 years/3), Biblical
Economic Crisis 2G to Economic Conspiracy -3G Span B.C. 1- A.D. 1970 years **>1666 years x3**
The formed of 3 Kingdoms,
Qing Dynasty (current Singapore) i.e. Commonwealth -A.D. 1616' -2G a.k.a. China Great Wall (Chinese-Western)
Democracy Revolution (current Taiwan) i.e. United Nations – A.D. 1910' -2.5G a.k.a. Berlin Wall (Poland-Germany)
Introduction Asia 4 Dragons (current Hongkong) i.e. Federation A.D. 1970' -3G a.k.a. Israel Wall (Christianity-Islam)

3G to 4G Canyon Road to Promised Land (Cold War Era 700 years/3), Quantum
Economic Conspiracy 3G to Economic Booming 4G A.D. 1000s-2000s **>700 years**
Invention of Pseudo Science, e.g. Printing Technology, i.e. Moveable Press, Steam Engine, Tungsten Light Bulb, AD. 1000s' – 3G
Discovery of Electromagnetic wave, e.g. Electrical Motor, Photo Camera, Radio, Sound Recorder, AD. 1800s' – 3.5G
Application of Economic Science, e.g. Digital Computer as well as Rocket Launched and Man Landing on Moon. AD. 1969' -4G

4G to 5G Silk Road to Oriental (Civil War Era 51 years/3), Pentecost

Economic Booming 4G to Economic Crisis – 5G 1970s-2020s **>50 year/2 x 2)**
Economic Booming, **Satan Released after 1000 years Prison**, *Civil War. AD. 1970' - 4.0G (Vietnam War, Myanmar War)(Buddhism vs Islam Schism), Application of 10 Commandment i.e. Victory Theology*

Station 1. First Resurrection – Oriental Express (Taiwan) i.e. Train (Pre-baptism)(Motorola 5G, 20 level private network)

1. Economic Crisis I, ***Advent Jesus***, *The Final Preaching to Oriental – A.D. 2000s' -4.5G (Persian Gulf War, Syrian War)(Islam & Christianity Schism,* **Fundamentalism***), Christian Science i.e. Calvinism Theology "The Apple".*
Jesus performs *"The Apple"* Salvation.
Mary to Raise all People & Creatures from 20th Level to 1st Level, and there are First Resurrection and First Dead.

2. Economic Crisis II, ***Devil, Beast and False Prophet were Judged to 18, 19, 20th Level*** *(AD. 2020s' -5G (Ukraine & Brazil)(Christianity & Hinduism Schism, Pentecostal), Prosperity Gospel i.e. Vision Theology "The Dark Magic"*

Station 2. Second Resurrection – Continental (Singapore) i.e. Car (Post-baptism)(Huawei 5G, 2x individual public network)

1i. *Economic Crisis III,* **Advent Christ***, (Christianity to Buddhism Schism,* **Episcopal***),* 2037' (United Kingdom War, China War), *Christology i.e. Salvation Theology "Another Heaven"*
Christ performs "Another Heaven" Salvation.
Father God to Judge Living and Dead from Heaven to Hell, and there are Second Resurrection and Second Dead.

2i. *Economic Crisis IV,* **False Christ, Satan, Man of Sins was judged to Hell together with other 2nd Dead***, (Christianity to Yoga Schism,* **Catholic***),* 2070' *(Australia War, Japan War), Mariology i.e. Anabaptism Theology "The Open Gate"*

G. Heaven Decryption Highlights 天堂解密标记

Disclaimer: Independent Production, reinvent, disclosure, reproduction not granted.
承诺: 独立制作, 重译, 转载, 翻录必究。

- **Heaven Decryption Part I,II,III,IV,V,VI,VII**
- **The Formed of Promised Land which is the End Product of Economy Booming**
- **The seeking of Oriental 3 keys.**
- **Two Time Line of Oriental**
- **The Fakebook to Promised Land and Oriental**

i. Heaven Decryption Part I,II,III,IV,V,VI,VII

Caution: The content included here contain highly misleading literature from Book of Revelation, that required supervision controlled. Read only if you are spiritual maturity enough accept the risk of being mind poisoned.

"Remember the Sabbath day by keeping it holy. Exodus 20:8

Part I. (The Code Decryption)

3 Coherent host contest themselves their own translator as well as reflection.
(War, Heaven),Guard the God Kingdom.
(United States,United Kingdom,Taiwan,Hongkong,Singapore,Australia)
quarantine/probe/mouth;SI System (United States)
e.g. English language and Mandarin language and/or Malay.
Continuous Spectrum (Ceramic,because of 5 color model,i.e.
red,blue,yellow,white,black)(Face feature)
流行歌 String 普通话 Data, Conjunction oriented – Fundamentalist Church – Mechanism – Formula (4D)
Face – Jesus vs Body – Trojan Horse

The rest **24 Series network** isolate their own translator as well as reflection.
(Advanced Civilisation, Paradise),Salvation to God Kingdom.
(Europe, Russia, China, Middle East)
jail/spy/eye;Imperial Unit (United Kingdom)
e.g. Germans Script, Russian Script, Chinese Script, Israel Script, Arabic Script.
Absorption Spectrum (Metallic,because of 4 color model,i.e.
red,blue,yellow,green)(Arts)
交响乐 Brass 文言文 Script, Vocabulary oriented – Episcopal Church – Textured – Code (5D)
Food – Messiah vs Book – Angel

18 Parallel network shared among their own translator as well as reflection.
(Promised Land, Hell),Crime Disruption.
(Africa,Thailand peninsular,Japan,Korea peninsular,South America,Indian Peninsular)
censorship/detain/ear;Metric System (Australia)
e.g. Pop song, Electronic music, Dance music, even Jazz music.
Emission Spectrum (Vivid,because of 3 color model,i.e. red,green,blue)(Nature)
儿歌 Guitar 白话文 Emoji, Preposition oriented – Pentecostal Church – Structured – Equation (3D)
Environment – Christ vs Social – E.T

Total 3 type of translator, distributed holistically. Namely B.C. before christ, A.D. after christ, C.E. common era. There are Avatar in all 45 network.1 out of 45 network is the True Avatar. The True Avatar can be in any 45 network, depend their affiliation and credit. 45 network has own physical, chemistry, biology, material model.

Those Election Ethnic or People are affiliated to 3 coherent host. These include 12 sect of Semitic, and those Country or Ethnic reconciliation with Islam as well as Semitic.
(Calvinism theology as well as Christianity foundation that build on Quran, God ethical road map)

Christian are undetermined belong to the rest 24 network, until the final judgement. It is Universal measurement, measure by 5 universal point.
The Scale is meaning realism, which is the gap standard between 18 parallel network and 3 coherent host.

In fact, 18 network are nearly close to 3 coherent host if using different judgement standard.
To change network, need connection (hope), affiliation (love) and credit (faith) and thru the manual mode.

Those appear censorship/detain/ear in the host are those in 18 parallel network.
Those appear jail/spy/eye in the host are those in 24 series network.
Those appear quarantine/probe/mouth in the host are those in 3 coherent network.

*If B.C. After Christ era, Satan will be go to Lower Ground the half hell, e.g. LG for 1000 years. Because of that, heaven can only reach half stage. If C.E. Common era, Devil and his gang will go to Basement the fire lake, that would be the 2nd dead. Only that, heaven can reach the full stage.

*By the way, all of these is the improvised of Christology Theology, in which constitute the fundamental for the Social Science, Mass Media and Telecommunication.

1. Capitalism; UN; Devil; Property Insurance; Life Insurance; News (Holding Opensource Technolog If Advanced Civilisation, there is **Tsunami** threat.
Newsletter: Fox, Telegraph, RT, **Sinchew, Zaobao,** CNA, **Shine**
Mustn't Instant, Mustn't Hub. Prevent fake news i.e. RSS; Prevent Manipulate prediction i.e. Archived.

2. GDP orientated; NATO; False Christ; Car Insurance; Communication (Terrorism activities)
If Crime Syndicate Disruption, there is **Terrorism** threat.
Message Hub: Twitter, **Facebook**, Whatsapp, **Wechat**, QQ, Telegram, Line, Weibo
Must Instant, Must Hub. Prevent secretive i.e. Typing status; Prevent Censorship i.e. History.

3. Communism; WWF; Satan; Social Insurance; Entertainment (Erotic Defect)
If Economic Transformation, there is **Erotic Conspiracy Crime** threat.
Matchmaking Agency: **Youtube**, **Tiktok**, Tinder, Pornhub
Mustn't Instant, Must Hub. Prevent artifact i.e. Streaming; Prevent Stealth i.e. Library.

4. Federalism; KMT; Serpent; Unemployment Insurance; Career (Social Disorder)
If Resurrection, there is **Virus Monetary Crime** threat.
Job Agency: Indeed, **Linkedin**
Mustn't Instant, Must Hub. Prevent Non serious advertising i.e. Deep Crawl; Prevent Non serious job seeker i.e. Comprehensive Database.

5. Gini orientated; NASA; Man of Sin; Liability Insurance; Religion (Gospel Leak & Misused)
If Advent of Heaven, there is **Abduction** threat.
Search Engine: WordPress, Bing, Google, **Yahoo, Baidu**, Blogspot
Mustn't Instant, Mustn't Hub. Prevent Boycott Website i.e. Deep Crawl; Prevent Public Safety i.e. Independent Ranking.

6. Commonwealth; WHO; False Prophet; Health Insurance; Disability Insurance; Food (Drug Abuse)
If Cultural Renaissance, there is **Nuclear** threat.
Online Delivery: **Foodpanda**, Grabfood, **Amazon, Taobao**, Ebay
Mustn't Instant, Mustn't Hub. Prevent Wrong Order i.e. Data Input; Prevent Keep Privacy Record i.e. Benchmark Statistic.

*Highlighted are those remarks as conspiracy.

Part II. (The Timeline Decryption)

- A.D. 1000s, Satan was captured and sent to assumed hell.
- A.D. 2000s, Satan released and Repented, but continued Tempting.
- A.D. 2000s, Devil and His Gangs were captured, send to hell.
- A.D. 3000s. First Batch of Champion of Galaxy who has their name in 'the book of life' join the assumed heaven, 'The 1st resurrection'.
- A.D. 4000s. The rest who doesn't has their name in the 'book of life' will join to the real heaven, 'The 2nd resurrection', it is believed following the True Jesus advent.

1st Beginning – Father God: Creator, World (The Draft version), Service Mark, Fundamental (Old Testament Combinative)
- Christian Science, CQ,IQ
  Eden Garden & Earth
  1 world contains, more than 36 and less than 45 civilisation. 36 to 45 Bible version. (The Draft version)

2nd Further – James: Created, Literature (The Improvised version), Copyright, Foundation (Prophet incl. Islam)
- Christian Music, AQ,CQ
  Bible & Quran
  Find out whichever Galaxy out of unlimited galaxy that contain the solar system, i.e. the son of God Jesus i.e. Tsunami. Hence 1 galaxy contain 9 out of 36 and/or less than 45 combinative civilisation.
  Rule out 1 Ultimate Quran version, which best describing the son of God. (The Improvised version)

3rd Subsequence – Mother Mary: Creating, Universe (The Beautified version), Trademark,
Legacy (Epistle incl. Paul)
- Christian Law, EQ,AQ
  Moon & Star
  Choose 7 set of remote solar system out of numbers of solar system and galaxy, that contain also black hole, Messiah i.e. Nuclear Bomb. Yield 7 Quran Annex Canon of Bible. (The Beautified version)

4th Foresee – Jesus: Creation, Machine (The Authentic version), Patent,
Pillar (Four Gospel incl. Canon)
- Christian Arts, AQ,CQ
  Computer & Car
  Rule out the Champion solar system and Champion Canon of Bible. (The Authentic version)

5th Final – Messiah: Creature, Heaven (The Ugly version), Open Source, Platform (Revelation incl. Every Numbers)

- Christian Mathematics, IQ,EQ
  Promised Land & Sky City
  Reorder the Champion of Galaxy, reorder the Champion of Canon of Bible. All mankind and living creature that has eternal life can live in heaven, and expected form. (The Ugly version)
- Jesus inheritor is not and not holding True Jesus identity.
- Jesus existed in every solar system but different form, so are we.
- Each galaxy with black hole has all their names written in the book of life, and non repeating.
- Other galaxy without black hole, doesn't has their names written in the book of life but has the grace of 'The 2nd Resurrection'.

1st Coming (Documentary)
True Jesus (A.D. 1s)

2nd Coming (Fictional)
NATO (Qing Syndicate, Asean) vs FBI (Communist, China)
Joshua vs James (Brother of True Jesus) (A.D. 1000s)

3rd Coming (Schism)
CIA (Federalism,Islam) vs UN (Capitalism,Commonwealth,Christianity) vs KMT (Communism,Buddhism)
James vs Nazareth vs Messiah (A.D. 2000s)

20 Combination
CIA,UN, & KMT Group

3rd Coming (False Christ)
NASA (Western or Asia)
James is Nazi Germany

Final Coming (Projection)
WWF, (Climate Change, Paris) vs WHO, (Global Warming, Copenhagen)
Santa Claus (A.D. 3000s) vs Christ (A.D. 4000s)

Part III. (The Religion Decryption)

Buddhism has wide civilisation and coverage, the hub of all philosophy.

Christianity is a platform in which for example the buddhism i.e Philosophy hub could be index, that has 4 view.
Christianity is the Fundamental, without platform, buddhism or philosophy alone without salvation.

Jesus is man and God. King of man. Matthew Gospel. Fundamentalist (Scientific).
Jesus is man. James. Mark Gospel. Episcopal (Impression).
Jesus not man and not God. Luke Gospel. Islam son of God Christ. Pentecostal (Meditating).
Jesus is son of God. Messiah. John Gospel. Catholic (Canon).

Pentecostal i.e. Lutheran is wicked. Protect Gospel Leak and bias to Islam.
Islam has their Rival of Jesus. Christ.

Alpha Nazareth would be the Son of God of Lutheran and Islam.

The official batch to heaven, incl. Pentecostal Church and Episcopal Church.
With Islam Platform. KMT
Advent of Heaven, awakening
Cold War. Crime Syndicate Disruption. Terrorism
e.g. 'The Fly', Tsunami (teleport) to A.D. 3000s.

Omega Messiah would be the Son or Daughter of God of Christianity and all Religion.

The certified batch to heaven, incl. Fundamentalist Church and Catholic Church
Wih Christianity Platform. UN
Resurrection, normal death
World War III. Economics transformation. Virus
e.g. 'Back to the Future', Nuclear (fast forward) to A.D. 4000s.

Part IV. (The Economy Decryption)

这是中世纪后 Post Middle Age 的文明。我们有安徒生，天方夜谭，红楼梦。不知不觉，白金汉宫文明已经来到了黄昏。

有药剂，兴奋剂，麻醉剂，维他命，疫苗，西医。有神学，钢琴，小提琴，圣乐。有涡轮发动机，火车，汽车，飞机，火箭，航天。有灯泡，留声机，相机，电脑，电话，卫星，稀土。人权党，民主党，工人党，政治学。牧羊人侦探学，心理健康教育，犹太主义经济学与创业学，管理学等。称为-后白金汉宫文明 Post Buckingham Civilisation。

五大工业的利与弊，知识工业，稀土工业，能源工业，数码工业，物流工业。新人类，世界大战，核武，器官买卖，恐怖炸弹。黑市，黑道渐渐应脱欧后绝迹。

取而代之的是次贷，逃税，逆向工程等商业欺诈。称为商业犯罪集团。

还有，与木马人 Trojan 的核武种族战争，与邪灵 Evil spirit 的气候经济冷战，与外星人 E.T 病毒科技大战。

随后是宗教以色列策略 Israel Diplomacy，气候变化防备计划 Climate Change Escape Plan，朝鲜半岛去核武化 Denuclearisation of Korea Peninsular，阴谋犯罪捣破 Conspiracy Crime Disruption，恐怖主义捣破 Terrorism Disruption。

Global Issue incl. White Supremacy & Anti-Semitic, Marriage Supremacy & Feminism, Auto-driving & Bullet Train, Digital Currency & Medicine Closed-source.

Economic Science incl. as below

Food: Five loaves and Two Fish make taste and hunger leverage.

Clothes: One size fit all, standardized Clothes promote E-Commerce and Internationalisation.

Household: Population census and Advanced Telecommunication.

Transport: Anti Noise Cancellation, Anti Pollutant, Enhanced Airbag, Emergency Escape.

Health: Closed-source Medicine demote Vaccine Platform, and Promote High Qualification Doctor.

Threat: Family oriented, build Architectural World City Icon. Migration crisis attract Pandemic, Poverty and Erotic derivative issues.

Entertainment: Virtual Reality VR Autobot, Augmented Reality AR Robotic, Artificial Intelligence AI Robot, sky is the limit.

Part V. (The Judgement Decryption)

Little Faith, Agnostic, Islam, Fundamentalist (Science), Jesus (Alpha), Son, Why, Basement
(Serpent, Burgerking)(Man of Sins, Subway)(Android, A.R., CQ)
(Capitalism, Economy Premises Country)(Promised Land)(Genetic Science, 火山, Nationalist)(Train 'A')
(Australia, Taiwan, Macao, Japan)(Middle East)(Brunei, Malaysia, Indonesia)
ZION (Moses Code)(High CQ)(Informative Processing)
CQ Mainstream: Capitalism, Attractive People,
Ministry Oriented. By Flesh alone. Science. For Man & Women (CQ).
Numbers: 16.66% Semitic, Islam, Fundamentalist
Thread, Law ->10 Index->Benchmark Hierarchy Height (Environment)->Promised Land i.e. Paradise
(Environment) 10 Index of Stability, (Limit by Heavy Weapon)(Pre-Judgement, Penalty)

Glorified & Marty, Christianity, Episcopal (Theology), Messiah, James, Children, Who, Center of Gravity
(Satan, Kentucky)(False Prophet, A&W)(Java, IoT, AQ)
(Oriental, Developed Country)(Heaven) (Quantum Science, 嫦娥, Monarchy)(Oriental Express Train)
(United Kingdom, Russia, Europe, Israel)(Singapore, North Korea)
NATO (Light Code)(High EQ)(Quantum Processing)
Core, Truth ->9 Algorithm->Bandwidth Vector (Spirit)->The Oriental i.e. Heaven
Sophisticated (Spirit) 2 Indicator of Spirit, a. Economy Loading, b. Audience Accuracy & Trials (Incentive or Tax)

Blind Faith, Multi-theism, Buddhism, Catholic (Law), Mary, Mother, Where, Mirror of Center of Gravity
(Devil, McDonald)(False Christ, Pizzahut)(Windows V.R., EQ)
(Third World, Infrastructure Country), (Upside Down World)(Digital Economy, 大白兔, Democracy)(Pirate Bay)
(Hongkong, South East Asia)(Italy, Spain, Portuguese)
UN (Hexagram Code)(High IQ)(Spatial Processing)
EQ Premium: Reborn, Considered People.
Charity Oriented. By Spiritual and Flesh. Arts. For Man, incl. Mainstream.
Numbers: 33.33% Egyptian, Buddhism, Episcopal
Count, Love ->2 Mode->Parametric Surface Warpage (Social)->Earth Village i.e. Back to Future
(Social) 2 Mode BackStage/On Air (Pro-Judgement, Credit Rating)

Atheism, Hinduism, Pentecostal (Mathematics), Jehovah, Father, When, Mirror of Top

(E.T.)(Linux, Cloud, AQ)

(United States)(South America, Africa, India, Korea)(Third World)

Monotheism, Lutheran, Eastern Orthodox (Engineering), Christ (Omega), Brother, What, Top of the Pyramid

(Transformer)(Apple A.I., IQ)

(China, East Europe, Egypt)(Oriental)

IQ Sand Box: Democracy, Understood by Nobody.

Serving oriented. By Spiritual alone. Music. For Women, incl Premium and Mainstream.

Numbers: 50% Himalayan, Hinduism, Pentecostal

Loop, Righteous ->3 Standard of Deviation of Tolerance->Assurance % e.g. Six Sigma (Craft)->Upside down World i.e. Hell

(Craft) 3 Batch Manual/Hybrid/Automatic (Post-Judgement, Mercy)

Great Eastern: Monarchy, Buddhism, Righteous, Episcopal: Singapore, United Kingdom, China, Russia

Oriental Pearl: Democracy, Hinduism, Truth, Pentecostal: Hongkong, United States, Korea, Poland

Continental: Capitalism, Islam, Law, Fundamentalist Taiwan, Australia, Japan, Belarus

Part VI. (The Bible Decryption)

Moses Law (Spiritual Miracle Research)
(The born of Israel)(1 loop 5000 years) 以色列的诞生之伊甸园
1 Man Split 1 Women (1 Land Split 1 Land)

Minor Prophets (Ethnic Research)
Moses Law variants
9 Ethnic (9 Regime)

Gospel Science (Science Research)
(Journey to the West)(1 loop 500 years) 西游记之应许之地
Chaos Theory->Economics Science->Religion Unity
Feedback Control->Computer Science->Church Reformation
Quantum Mechanics->Material Science->Industrial Revolution
Genetic Matrix Computation->Biological Science->Cultural Renaissance
4 Era (4 Majesty)

Apostle Letters (Theology Research)
Gospel Science variants
9 Kingdom (9 Theology)

Revelation (Holy Spirit Research)
(Final Destination)(1 loop 5 years) 东游记之东方之珠
5 Church (5 Land)

Continental – (Dragon)(4 Creatures)(333 Place)-(2 Religion)
Oriental Pearl – (Antichrist)(999 Place)(7 Dream Godness)-(9 Ethnic)
New Babylon – (Beast)(7 Whistle)(24 Angel Guardian)-(4 Era)
Great Eastern – (False Prophet)(666 Place)(7 Disaster)-(9 Church)
New Jerusalem – (Serpent a.k.a. Man of sins)(12 type of fruits)(10 Kings)-(5 Land)

Part VII. (The Ultimate Decryption of Heaven)

United States King James version: James->Advocate Accomplishment of Law
(Guided of Endeavour, Consecutive)(Imperialism)(Future Sin)
Germany, Step 2a. Earth Village, Free loops->1000 years
Salvation African, (India, America)
Fascism: Pentecostal i.e. Lutheran (Pseudo Science) vs Transformer (Social Science)
Goal: Validation of Four Gospel->Christian Education
Game over: Adultery induce (Terrorism). (False Prophet)(Hongkong)(Israel)(Mafia
Fund I)
Reward: Vatican (Italy)

United Kingdom: English Standard version: Messiah->Advocate Demonstration of
Law (Credit of Love, Properties)(Popularism)(Past Sin)
Russia, Step 1. Heaven, Free loops->5000 years
Salvation Atheist (Thai, Asia)
Nazism: Episcopal (Information Management) vs Grey (Applied Physics)
Goal: Demonstration of Legacy of Four Gospel->Hymn Preaching
Game over: Cult induce Tsunami and Nuclear. (Beast)(Hongkong)(Israel)(Jail
Terrorism Guardian)
Reward: Buckingham Palace (United Kingdom)

Taiwan: Chinese Union version: Jesus->Advocate Constitution of Law (Category of
Law, Hierarchy)(Nationalism)(Original Sin)
Israel, Step 2b. Promised Land, Free loops->500 years
Salvation Egyptian (Germanic, Germans)
Marxism: Eastern Orthodox i.e. Fundamentalist Presbyterian (Politic Science) vs E.T.
(Rocket Science)
Goal: Implementation Moses 10 Law Commandment in Politics->Economy Science
Game over: Poverty induce Tsunami then Nuclear.
(Dragon)(Germany)(Russia)(Pentecostal Fund)
Reward: Military Alliance (Russia)

China: Chinese Standard version: Christ->Advocate Application of Law (Omni of
Truth, Free)(Chauvinism)(Present Sin)
Hongkong, Step 3. Oriental, Free loops->40 years
Salvation Chinese (Diaspora, Main City)
Fusionism: Catholic i.e. Fundamentalist Methodist (Crime Network Channel) vs
Predator (Earth Science)
Goal: Application of 10 Law Commandment in Theology->Crime Disruption
Games over: Random Judgement induce Ethnic Genocide Epidemic. (False
Christ)(Germany)(Russia)(Mafia Fund II)
Reward: White house (United States)

All Four Steps must automated then sorted to form an individual Alpha-Omega
Time Line.
Those time line are then merged into A to Z Time Line.

1. Capitalism; UN; Devil; Property Insurance; Life Insurance; News (Holding Opensource Technolog If Advanced Civilisation, there is **Tsunami** threat.
Newsletter: Fox, Telegraph, RT, **Sinchew, Zaobao,** CNA, **Shine**
Mustn't Instant, Mustn't Hub. Prevent fake news i.e. RSS; Prevent Manipulate prediction i.e. Archived.

2. GDP orientated; NATO; False Christ; Car Insurance; Communication (Terrorism activities)
If Crime Syndicate Disruption, there is **Terrorism** threat.
Message Hub: Twitter, **Facebook**, Whatsapp, **Wechat**, QQ, Telegram, Line, Weibo
Must Instant, Must Hub. Prevent secretive i.e. Typing status; Prevent Censorship i.e. History.

3. Communism; WWF; Satan; Social Insurance; Entertainment (Erotic Defect)
If Economic Transformation, there is **Erotic Conspiracy Crime** threat.
Matchmaking Agency: **Youtube, Tiktok**, Tinder, Pornhub
Mustn't Instant, Must Hub. Prevent artifact i.e. Streaming; Prevent Stealth i.e. Library.

4. Federalism; KMT; Serpent; Unemployment Insurance; Career (Social Disorder)
If Resurrection, there is **Virus Monetary Crime** threat.
Job Agency: Indeed, **Linkedin**
Mustn't Instant, Must Hub. Prevent Non serious advertising i.e. Deep Crawl; Prevent Non serious job seeker i.e. Comprehensive Database.

5. Gini orientated; NASA; Man of Sin; Liability Insurance; Religion (Gospel Leak & Misused)
If Advent of Heaven, there is **Abduction** threat.
Search Engine: WordPress, Bing, Google, **Yahoo, Baidu**, Blogspot
Mustn't Instant, Mustn't Hub. Prevent Boycott Website i.e. Deep Crawl; Prevent Public Safety i.e. Independent Ranking.

6. Commonwealth; WHO; False Prophet; Health Insurance; Disability Insurance; Food (Drug Abuse)
If Cultural Renaissance, there is **Nuclear** threat.
Online Delivery: **Foodpanda**, Grabfood, **Amazon, Taobao**, Ebay
Mustn't Instant, Mustn't Hub. Prevent Wrong Order i.e. Data Input; Prevent Keep Privacy Record i.e. Benchmark Statistic.

*Highlighted are those remarks as conspiracy.

ii. The Formed of Promised Land which is the End Product of Economy Booming

New Jerusalem, Taiwan, Christian Persecution (Australia, Germany), Fundamentalist Church, Nationalism (Christianity, Trinity), Heaven, Terrorism Syndicate, Full Picture Montage & Global Versed, False Christ versus Jesus a.k.a. Christian Scientist

New Judah, Singapore, Jail Terrorism (Russia, Japan), Catholic, Monarchy (Hinduism, Monotheism), Judgement, Organised Conspiracy Syndicate, Legacy & Diplomatic Strategy, Beast versus Mary a.k.a. Monalisa

New Canaan, China, Anti Semitic (United States, Korea), Pentecostal Church, Democracy (Buddhism, Atheism), Justice, War Syndicate, Copyright Law & Network Union, Dragon versus Jehovah a.k.a. James Bond

New Bethlehem, Malaysia, Erotic Defect (United Kingdom, Italy), Episcopal Church, Liberalism (Islam, Multi-theism), Salvation, Mafia, Theology & Education, False Prophet versus Christ a.k.a. God Father

The Four Orthogonal Direction, Heaven (left), Salvation (right), Justice (up), Judgement (down) formed a Typical Cross.

The Vector Pictorial represented the dynamics of revolution i.e. Holy Spirit. The are many combination e.g. European Country Flags. This is also can think of analogy of Islam Logo in Arabic script.

The correct proportional parameter i.e. Vector Pictorial significant the Miracle yielded Promised Land, the God Election Continent. It is the place where diplomatic strategy Christianity and Islam, and also the end product of Economy Booming, the Abundant of Life activities. The Promised Land heading to Oriental i.e. The Real Heaven by then.

Time line to Real Heaven required 1000 years as recorded in Book of Revelation. The Promised Land is the long journey, depend on the Icon of Cross.

The Holy Spirit as well as the Human Evolution, define the Icon of Cross. The Doctrine & Theology translated from Maturity of Holy Spirit. The Human Evolution relating to Universe Expansion limited by the Social Disorder i.e. Civilisation.

Noted that Advanced Civilisation limited by God Ethic i.e. 10 Law of Commandment Hierarchy, rule of thumb, e.g. the Abundant Material Technology with Limited Quantum Technology, Limited Digital Technology but Strictly No Genetic Science.

iii. The seeking of Oriental 3 keys.

It had to be in United, All three or four which are Law within Love, Love within Truth, and Truth within Hope. The greatest is Hope.

Holy Spirit from Grace, Holy Spirit from Gift and Holy Spirit from Burden. Episcopal talk about Grace, Fundamentalist talk about Gift, and Pentecostal talk about Burden. Catholic talk about Spiritual Body. Without Burden, i.e. Freedom, all vain.

There is obstacle to Spiritual Body, due to the Marriage Defects. And Genetic expression. The Genetic expression depend on Human Evolution along with the Universe Linear Expansion. The Superman.

That is from Social Circle Bonding Scale. Analogy to Harddisk Defragment. Or simply the plain geographical area.
That is promised Land. The End Time era.

Many combinations, it could be World War combination to Advanced Civilisation. West and East. The Montage depend on Church Revolution. Its about Doctrine and Theology.

The Astronomy, Social Science, Ethnic, Genetic Histogram, Mathematics, Quantum Computation. The are no more than 9 Graded Theology. Its analogy to the Solar system. Its more toward Computer Science, called Algorithm.

Spiritual Body is Longitudinal Wave, the Sound the Matter. The Radiant is Quantum property. Promised Land is not the final destination. The direction is Oriental, from Physical Body to Spiritual Body. Pro Photon Histogram i.e. Geometric to Pro Quantum States i.e. Material Property. That what we can expect in the major progression from Promised Land to Oriental.

The route of time line is series to parallel. Many Oriental in contested. The Contest of Ultimate Theology and the Ultimate Ethnic. That must be aligned to Religion Election People. e.g. Islam Egyptian, Christianity Chinese and Common Semitics. That is called 2nd resurrection and 2nd Judgement. Destined but non specific. Christ-mas. And Anti Christ.

Its not good to get Theology Insight, as this is considered Cheating. No cheating to Baptism. Its not open door. How skillful of your theology. The key is the Marriage Law and Family Salvation. That is past generation and future generation. The seeking of the Supernova as top hierarchy. It is the search algorithm. Called Calvinism Theology. The undelete algorithm is the Christology Theology. In which Revert the pre-justice by Marriage Defects cause by next generation. The genetic expression.

All of the theology is about quality control methodology. e.g. Six Sigma. Nothing to learn, but avoid. Choose as many as you can, no gift. From Climate it may be revealed. It ought to Revolution of Theology to match the regenerated Holy Spirit and renewable Spiritual Body. It form the Basis of the Oriental where we heading to. Which is Marriage (for girl) and Family (for man). Make sure facing upward, not downward.

Family salvation is the very critical topics. Not using Theology method, but Power of Holy Spirit. Theology method should be remained as VIP, no leaked. But Christian Education. must be as Public and copyrighted. a.k.a. Agnostic Education, this is an open door to eternal life.

Holy Spirit is language instead of science. We have to start as early as Kindergarten. That's the different of Science and Mathematics. So teaching Mathematics is as difficult as teaching Music. That is the limitation of Power of Holy Spirit, comes from the Informatics. It has to be cleanses by Fire and Lake.

The Righteousness, Forgiveness, Perseverance, Holiness play critical role as Blind Love, Blind Faith, and Blind Hope.
Blind is the scale, Wisdom is the blessing. Give and Take. It doesn't work either way cheating.

Be careful of the derivative of Holy Spirit. Its not bear fruits, if no burden. Burden of Holy Spirit limited by Marriage Law and Family Salvation. Comes as Marriage Burden and Family Burden. Heal the past and shape the future.
In Own Family Context. This is Imperialism. And that is the perfect answer to Burden of Holy Spirit. The Spirit of Satan, Serpent or Devil.

iv. Two Line of Oriental

Economy/God will (Agape Love)->Nationalism (Islam, Agnostic Islam, Presbyterian) or Republican (Buddhism, Fundamentalist, Catholic)->Continental (Difficult)

God will/Economy (Marriage Love)->Royalism (Christianity, Alpha-Omega) or Monarchy (Hinduism, Partial-theism)->Oriental Pearl (Challenge)

Grace of God (Family Love)->Imperialism (Christianity, Mafia Syndicate) or Vatican (Hinduism, Conspiracy Syndicate)->Great Eastern (Normal)

Population (Plato Love)->Democracy (Islam, Atheism, Terrorism Syndicate) or Communism (Buddhism, Multi-theism, War Syndicate)->Oriental (Easy)

Rule of Game:

There 4 category, in which rely on 4 different power, e.g. Economy power, God will power, Population power, and Grace of God power.

First thing first, each group objective is to beat off all the rest of 7 groups to gain victory. or Allied.

To start with Population power, it has two division Democracy and Communism, in which Democracy is to protect the Dragon, the **Idolatry Model leader** as whole objective to victory. But Communism objective is to **against the idol**.

2nd, God will power, to continued with Royalism main objective is to development of God will from the Theology Research supplementary with Islam God will, at the same time, protect the **Alpha and Omega**, the Jesus inheritor and Christ inheritor.

3rd, The Monarchy is to time searching the Joshua a.k.a. Messiah, the leader of Mass Preaching, at the same time development the alternative of **God will** from the Theology Research.
3rd, Economy power, the Nationalism main objective is to Reinvent of **Economy Science** Foundation from Politic, Ethnic, Music, etc. Social Science, combine with Scientific Theology to gain victory in Economy Booming ultimately. The Republican is to against this by Inventing the **Rocket Science** Pillar to gain Economy Booming.

4th, Grace of God power, the Imperialism objective is to **get judgement & justice**. The Vatican is to oppose Imperialism objective, by **Holy Spirit Research**.

"Do not judge, or you too will be judged. Matthew 7:1
"不要评断人，免得你们被评断。马太福音 7:1

List of Group of Organization:

1. Nationalism KMT, Taiwan, Germany (Nuclear)(Monitor)

2. Republican NASA, China, Australia (Virus)(Secretary)

3. Royalism WWF, New Zealand, Singapore

4. Monarchy WHO, United Kingdom, Malaysia

5. Imperialism NATO, Russia, France

6. Vatican CIA, Hongkong, Italy (Tsunami)(Mastermind)

7. Democracy UN, United States, Korea (Terrorism)(Fund)

8. Communism FBI, Vietnam, Israel

Axis
Group A. (Agnostic)(Industrial Revolution)
Taiwan, Germany, Malaysia (Earth Village, Clock wise)
Group B. (Pentecostal)(Christianity Reformation)
France, Hongkong, Korea, United States, Vietnam (Hell, Anti Clockwise)

Allied
Group A. (Fundamentalist)(Economy Booming)
Australia, Singapore, New Zealand, China, United Kingdom (Promised Land, Jumping Time)
Group B. (Catholic)(Renaissance)
Russia, Italy, Israel (Heaven, Time Still)

*The Scale depend on the maximum bandwidth in the heaven.

v. The Fakebook to Promised Land and Oriental

Righteous, Forgiveness, Patience is Fundamentalist Christianity Principle. Forgiveness, Perseverance, Verification, Holiness is Islam Principle of True Love. Christianity Theology use Risk Management i.e. Science. And Islam use Energy Management i.e. Economy. Science is for Trinity God, Economy is for Multi-Theism. With Lever effect, these going to Works for many of us.

There is Buddhism variant has many content of Principle of True Love. All of those Buddhism are experimental Science.

And of these named as the Dimension of Science. Experimental is Fun. It got to synergy all of these for New Age Religion.

Without Agnostic Fundamentalist Church without Promised Land. Without New Age Religion without the Oriental.

There are New Babylon Promised Land and New Canaan Promised Land. There are Oriental Pearl, Continental, or Great Eastern for Real Heaven.

The Hope is Principle, Love is Law, Faith is Theory. The Greatest is Law. Never do the application of the 10 Commandment Law, it is non legit. As Love and 10 Commandment is a Hierarchy. People do so always infringe the 1st greatest commandment.

Academically, Love is for Family and Social, and Faith is for Country and Ethnic, Hope is for Marriage & Ministry.
Never Experimental or Application of Love to Family and Social but strictly follow and adhere the 10 Commandment of Moses. In doing so, you have good Network Rating Score i.e. Pre-judgmental Score. And that would be our daily foods and entertainment. Called Economics. Economics is homogeneous, & whole universe.

When the Promised Land formed up, we will relocated to new earth, there is only single phase of time, one direction progression. Thats meant perfect world. That would be Multi-theism, e.g. Alpha-Omega Theology, or Mario-logy Theology. The Perfect world for imperfect Spirit, there would be more testing, trials and temptation as record in Book of Revelation.

For those route the Shortcut to Heaven e.g. Oriental, could had skip Testing, Trials and Temptations. These all called "The Fakebook to Promised Land and Oriental." From the argument of Economy Science and Modern Theology". The legacy is from the Reformed Church Theology and My Own Version Bible Translation. For those read the Fakebook, your Economy as well as Life Expectancy affected, due to the High Pre-judgmental Score. Give and Take.

Glossary

Timeline of end world: Zigzac, and anytime.

Mastermind: Racist related, not money related for sure.

Marriage Supremacy: Non Specific Marriage, preferential on Bread over Love. Advocate Testimony.

Marriage Autonomy: Specific Marriage, preferential on Love over Bread. Advocate Ministry.

Political Wing: Far left point to conservative, far right point to radical.

Superstitious: Crime Disorder, Erotic, Heresy, Multi-theism, e.g. Crime.

Idealism: Economy Disorder, Idealism, Serve two God, Trinit-ism e.g. Terrorism.

Materialism: Social Disorder, Secular, No Righteous, Monotheism, e.g. Raping.

Popularism: Civil Disorder, Nationalism, Idolism, Agnostic, e.g. Fraud.

Marxism: Marxism, Far Left wing, Socialism.

Fusionism: Fusionism, Centre Left wing, Religionism.

Nazism: Far Right wing, Materialism.

Fascism: Fascism, Centre Right wing, Racialism.

Neo Nazi: Economy Disorder as well as Anti-Chinese. Enterprise Syndicate incl. Qing Syndicate. Anti-Chinese.

Fasci Japan: Civil Disorder as well as Anti-God. Crime Syndicate incl. East India Company. Qing Regime.

Nazi Germany: Social Disorder as well as Anti-Semitic. War Syndicate. Anti-Semitic. Soong Sister Dynasty.

Communist Crime Disorder as well as Anti-Christ. Terrorism Syndicate incl. Islamic State. Qing Conspiracy Basement.

Russian Bratva: Linkup to Taliban & Mind Control Society. Custom Committee.

East India Company: Linkup to Al-Qaeda & Casino Society. Hospital Committee.

Klu Klux Klan: Linkup to ISIS & Mental Research Institute. Casino Committee.

Italy Mafia: Linkup to Islamic State & Falungong syndicate. Bank Committee.

IQ: Intelligence Quotient, Identity, Statistical.

AQ: Adversity Quotient, Thing, Parameter.

CQ: Creative Quotient, Time, Directional.

EQ: Emotional Quotient, Place, Geometrical.

Goal Oriented: Two-way thinking. Versus analysis. Duality.

Task Oriented: Alternative way thinking. Brainstorming. One direction.

Result Oriented: Multiple-way thinking. Independent analysis. Concurrent.

Process Oriented: One-way thinking. Critical analysis. Sequence.

Nationalism: Three party formation a.k.a. 3 People's Principle. Human Right inclined. e.g. Protestation.

Pan Democracy: Alliance formation, Coverage inclined. e.g. Money Campaign.

Democracy: Coalition formation, Two party political formation. Credit Inclined. e.g. Presidential Election.

Republican: One party formation. Population inclined. e.g. General Election.

Federalism: Slaved & Commercial Crime inclined. Charity model. Government Monetary.

Commonwealth: Erotic & Intelligence Crime inclined, Labour inclined. Investment model. Family Monetary.

Capitalism: Labour & Criminal Crime inclined. Supply Chain model. Individual Monetary.

Communism: Servicing & Civil Crime, Servicing inclined. Franchised model. Partial Government Monetary.

Reunification of Religion: Oppose to Renaissance. Religion Unity. Economy Recession. Shia Islam commission, e.g. Babylon.

Economics transformation: Oppose Industrial Revolution. Economy Booming. Agnostic Islam commission, e.g. Nile River.

Cultural Renaissance: Belong to Social Disorder. No racial discrimination and racial reconciliation but Anti-Semitic. Economy Downturn. Sufism Islam commission, e.g. Aegean Sea.

Industrial Revolution: Technology foundation as well as infrastructure upgrading. Economy Crisis. Sunni Islam commission, e.g. Babel Tower.

Jew 3 tribes: Zion i.e. Irish, Hebrew i.e. Jew, Semitic i.e. Jude.

Semitic 12 sects: Any ethnic pre-selection for salvation among each racial formed the definition of Semitic 12 sects. e.g. Israel, Hongkong, Dubai, New Delphi, total 12 sects.

Copyright: Foundation, Improvised version.

Patent: Pillar, Authentic version.

Copycat: Platform, Ugly version.

Trademark: Legacy, Beautified version.

Service Mark: Fundamental, Draft version.

Improvised: a.k.a. Jazz, Original Chord, Advertisement Music. incl. Poetry song.

Retro: a.k.a. Folk, Original Melody, Sheet Music. incl. Church song.

Indie: a.k.a. Pop, Original Tone, Album Music. incl. Christmas song.

Unplugged: a.k.a. Rock, Original Tempo, Concert Music. incl. Hymn song.

Classical: a.k.a. Symphony, Original Rhythm, Recording Music. incl. Praise song.

Dali 大理: Suspended Scale. Indian, Mainland Chinese 华夏民族, incl. 闽, 澳, 台

Dunhuang 敦煌: Harmonic Minor Scale. Chosen, Diaspora Chinese 中华民族, incl. 津, 港, 新

Shangri La 香格里拉: Diminished Scale. Korean, National Chinese 大汉民族, incl. 浙

Green Island 绿岛: Harmonic Major Scale. Japanese, Mandarin Chinese 大华民族, incl. 京, 苏, 粤

Dagger 小刀会: Augmented Scale. Thai, Oversea Chinese 华侨民族, incl. 桂, 蒙

Broadway: 1 per Bass, Portuguese incl. African, Portuguese

Quartet: 4 per Strings, Spanish incl. Jude, Greek, Spanish

Band: 3 per Choir, French incl. Germanic, Irish, French

Accompany: 2 per Piano, Dutch incl. Celt, Dutch

Orchestra: 5 per Drum, Italian incl. Jew, Italian

Boiled; Baked: Pork & Seafood, South America, Macao, Nanjing.

Steamed; Stew: Mutton & Venison, Europe, Taiwan, Tianjin.

Stir Fry; Roasted: Poultry & Vegetable, Australia, Malaysia, Shanghai.

Fried; Grill: Fish & Egg, United Kingdom, Hongkong, Beijing.

Braised; Gravy: Beef & Duck, United States, Singapore, Shenzhen

Chinese Medicine: Therapy e.g. Acupuncture.

Drug: Herbs e.g. Supplementary.

Vaccine: Cures e.g. Immune.

Pharmacy: Tonics e.g. Nutriology.

Quarantine Management: Testing e.g. Laboratory.

Regenerative Medicine: Chinese Medicine, New Age Medicine, Psychiatry Drug, Herbs, Therapy Oriented.

Nutriology Medicine: Western Medicine, Surgical Medicine, Pharmacy Supplement, Tonics, Anatomy Oriented.

Hexagram Code Numeric, Cipher, Superimposed, Chronicle to Name Etymology.

Morse Code Alphabet, String, Thread, Festival to Name Etymology.

Light Code Symbol, Echo, Histogram, Capital to Name Etymology.

Theorem: Business Management, Telecommunication, Pseudo Science; Commission.

Theory: a.k.a. Law, Astronomy, Arts, Applied Physics, Nature Science; Ethic.

Theology: a.k.a. Canon, Politics, Risk Management, Operation Management, Social Science; Spirit.

Doctrine: a.k.a. Principle, Medicine, Music, Logistic, Architecture Science; Ethnic.

Dogma: a.k.a. Theory, Martial Arts, War Strategic, Criminology, Psychology; Erotic.

Principle: Genealogy and Medicine. a.k.a. Bible Character. i.e. Ethnic.

Law: Archaeology and Astronomy. a.k.a. Bible Story i.e. Ethic.

Catechism: Constitutions and Politics. a.k.a. Canon of Bible.

Justice: Criminal Law and Anti-Social Law, against Crime Disorder i.e. Criminal Justification.

Justification: Holy Confession, Forgiveness, Faith, Speak in tongue.

Sanctification: Holy Baptism, Repentance, Love, Pentecost.

Glorification: Holy Communion, Offering, Hope, Theosis.

Regeneration: Holy Sacrament, Righteousness, Work, Christian Perfection.

Testimony: Its harms than benefit, do ministry than testimonial for Orthodox Christianity nor for Atheism.

Orthodox Christianity: Apostolic Church where Ministry of God as well as Missionary is valued. Teaching of Overview and strengthening of Christianity Fundamental.

Lutheran: Churches that value Salvation by Faith alone as well as value 'No racial discrimination', it is disrupting social harmony if too vigorous. Teaching of Basic and strengthening Christianity Foundation.

Christianity Reforming: Separating Lutheran Church out of four division of Christianity denomination.

Trinity: One to Three, Three entity regulated to Core.

Monotheism: Three in One, Three core regulated to one entity.

Erotic Defect: Man or women whoever compromise sex before and/or after marriage.

Adultery: Man or women pursuit love for money or pursuit love for sex before and/or after marriage.

Evil Spirit: Whoever contributing to social disorder as well as strong will of destruction conscious holistically.

Anti-Semitic: Link to Nazi Germany, in which any illegal activities contributed to disrupting Jew as well as those Pre-selection Jew from each racial group, for reconciliation.

Religion Unity: Link to Christianity Reforming, the endeavour of Orthodox Christianity to form alliance with Islam as well as other Orthodox religion.

Heaven: Link to Social Disorder, the place called itself heaven is the place where no social disorder and forward to progressive high civilisation and to perpetual life.

Christian Science: Conclude in Scientific theology as well as Creationism belief, a.k.a. Fundamentalist.

Pseudo Science: Conclude in Telecommunication as well as Revelation belief, a.k.a. Pentecostal.

Salvation: Those who are Completed Christian as well as those who equip with Christianity equivalent methodology. There is no single way but many ways led to salvation.

Canon: The rule in and rule out of targeted number of books from Old Testament as well as from New Testament to form an interconnected logical loop in other to fulfil the teachings of Salvation of Christ.

Climate Disaster Readiness: Conspiracy of Tsunami, targeting to block the evangelism of Christianity as well as targeting disrupt human civilisation by minimising the global emergency readiness in all activities to disperse human connection e.g. Social Disorder, Anti-Semitic, Religion disharmony, Terrorism, Erotic defect, World War.

Nuclear Weapon: High destructive, low occurrence nuclear weapon, literally it has no threatening advantage over other mass destructive weapon. But it can be illegally misused out of control the crude oil economy as well as preventive measure of escalating to World war.

Social Disorder: Link to Nazi Germany, in which a society harmony is disrupted in terms of social connection as well as social affiliation on weighing to leader of society.

Social Security: Liability on privacy/freedom that cause threat, depends on social sensitivity, popularism & social ranking mismatched i.e. social disorder.

Semitic Persecution: Social Disorder Activity, incl. Quarantine, Job sanction. Same to Christian Persecution.

Upstream technology: Fundamental/Innovative technology rely on academic.

Downstream technology: Foundation/Frontier technology rely on experiment.

Health Law: i.e. Systematic Biology a.k.a. Robot Technology, Hardware. 12 symbol, 12 Robot Organs as well as 12 Human Organs corresponding to 12 Chemistry Compound, incl. 3 Energy Mechanism.

Psychology Law: i.e. Systematic Psychology. a.k.a. Robot Technology, Software. Intelligence, Emotional, Creative and Adversity Quotient. incl. Scalar Computer, e.g. Measuring software, Quantum Computer, e.g. Solver software.

Pharmacy: Enzymes, Hormones, Mucosa, Insulin corresponding to Stem cell, Vitamin, Analgesic, Steroid.

Artificial Intelligence: Technology about Automation and Robot. If Civilisation reach peak, beyond that would bring humanity destruction, point to Medicine Science and Telecommunication Science.

Augmented Reality: Technology about Machine and Robotic. If Civilisation reach a stalled situation, above that would bring humanity advanced, point to Logistic Science and Combustion Science.

Virtual Reality: Technology about Simulation and Computer. If Civilisation reach crisis, below that would bring humanity downturn, point to Engineering and Computer Science.

Economy Load: Quantity of Mainstream Population, as High quantity of Mainstream population comes along reduced Economy Bill.

Mainstream population: The Bandwidth of telecommunication is the measure of Mainstream population.

Life expectancy: The measure of telecommunication bandwidth of a person, point to their endervour, ministry and life expectancy.

Harvest Gain Theory: i.e. Calendar Theory, a.k.a. Relativity Theory. The relationship of (Bandwidth of telecommunication)^power of X/(Half-life) proportional to (Harvest Gain). Analogy from Farmers and Fisherman. Half-life is a constant, but it depends on the gravitational field, i.e. moon phase. These contributed to Operation Management e.g. Agriculture, Food.

Chaos Theory: i.e. Time progression Theory, a.k.a. Entropy Theory, 2 way time progression, Closed form system, Predictable, Entropy, series events, Automatic Guiding, End loops, Analogy from Combustion Science. These contributed to Transportation e.g. Satellite, Jet.

Reality Decryption Theory: i.e. Augmented Reality Theory a.k.a. Feedback Control Theory, Algorithm Engine (Sensor, Encryptor) transfer to Combustion Engine (Actuator, Synthesizer) then to Film Engine (Gauge, Decryptor), Analogy from Computer Science. These contributed to Augmented Reality e.g. Mining, Construction, Nuclear Reactor etc.

Light Code Theory: i.e. Time Phase Theory a.k.a. Engineering Drafting Theory, 4 Distance Formula of 9 Planet, yield Hexagram Code to Moses Code then to Light Code. i.e. Metric system to Imperial system then to International Unit. These contributed to Engineering e.g. Telecommunication, Manufacturing.

Inheritance Decryption: There are Long generation, Wide generation interpolated to Orphanage generation, Broken generation and Ancient generation, which stick to inherited of father or mother gene. This constitutes to the fundamental of medicine, called contagious disease.

Rocky Effect Decryption: There is a guarantee that mainstream will always remain constant, if there is guarantee victory; it has to uphold anything what confirmed and assured into equation of fighting. This constitutes to the fundamental of manufacturing, called quality management.

Heaven Decryption: No more than 45 network. 3 network is coherent host. Each network has own translator as well as reflection. 18 same of a kind parallel network, 24 isolated series networks. This constitutes to the fundamental of social science, called mass media.

About Croyalflush Ministry Foundation 关于活石事工基金会

Caution: Some scam disguised Cult as Online Church. Prohibited worshiping Online Church, even with Covid-19 Epidemic, don't follow the trend, please take Spiritual carefully. No one can worship God without Tabernacleand without Fellowship.

"..You shall not take the name of the LORD your God in vain…" Exodus 20:1-17

Disclaimer: We are a Profit Organisation, rooted in Adelaide, Melbourne, Klang, Singapore, and Established in Johor Bahru. We very much like a Christian School as well as a Christian Solution Consultancy. We had accumulated certain extent of experiences & knowledge-base from Practical in Engineering, Politic, Music, Criminology, Theology, Economic, and Christian Education incl. Christian Mathematics, Christian Arts, Christian Science, Christian Music and Christian Law. We are serving upstream God Ministry and selectively downstream public ministry, e.g. Product Invention, Politic Revolution Campaign, Music Show, Crime Disruption Project, Theology Publication etc. You may find us in High Level teaching as close as Christian School by Christian Education Heritage. You may find us in High Level problem resolve as good as Christian Solution Consultancy in solving the real world Economic Science Development Issue. We are highly efficient, with nearly zero funding, we managed struggle to success, but with your devoted or little donation would shape us in many ways to sustain or speedy heading to victory against wicked power and evil network.

- About Croyalflush Ministry Foundation, 关于活石事工基金会

A. Our Vision:

Preserved Scientific Theology. i.e. Building the **Religion Unity Pillar**.

B. Our Mission:

Economic Science Research to Exit Federalism the Ecosystem Economic. i.e. **Salvation to whole Chinese Ultimately**.

C. Our Job:

Promote Long Hierarchy Company & Revealed as well as Opposed all kind of Christian Persecutions. i.e. **Advent of God Kingdom Decryption**.

D. Our Ministry:

Guideline to Disruption Climate Change Conspiracy. i.e. **Advanced Civilisation Threshold**.

E. Our Organisation & Milestone:

E1. Christian Education Aggregate
Published 'Fundamental of Christianity' website for Evangelism to Non believer and Reformation for Reborn Christian by Christian Science.

E2. Theology Aggregate
Published 'Matthew Gospel Commentary', 'New Theology Application' , 'Six Bible Myth', 'Nine Portion of Theology' Articles.

E3. Criminology Aggregate
Published 'End World Backup Plan' Book content incl. Crime Syndicate Network Revealed & Christian Persecution Revealed & Crime Conspirator Disruption Guide.

E4. Economic Aggregate
Published 'Light Encyclopedia™, Book total 700 Pages, content incl. Culture Heritage, Religion, Applied Physics, Social Science to Economic Science.

E5. Music Aggregate
Published CroyalPiano™ Music Encyclopedia, variety of Arrangement and Composed Music & Song. incl. Chinese Classic, Korean Pop, Piano Theme, Hymn Retro.

E6. Politic Aggregate
Published 'Editorial Articles' of each Country issue as well as Global Issue, to reach Ministry Agenda.

E7. Engineering Aggregate
Published CroyalDesign™ Machine Gallery incl. Cleared Leading Design & Manufacture Milestone for making Travel Gadget Grade Mobile Phone, Kitchen Appliance Grade P.O.S. Computer and Business Instrument Grade Meter.

F. Join Us

We are just small scale Educator & Consultancy Organisation, to survive we ought to grow up to moderate organisation for gaining power and influences. There are many phase and way you can join. If you saw this notice and feel interested please don't hesitate contact the Croyalflush Ministry Foundation's Secretary for delivering your interest, and there are alot of new jobs can be assigned.

Those Organization or Individuals who had partnership or contributes, this is the remembrance. We much care for any mis-leading or fallibility of Religion Belief, if yes, please let us know before you make report and take necessary action against us. Thank you!

The harvest is plentiful but the workers are few. Matthew 9:37
收割的工作多，而工人少。马太福音 9:37

About Founders 关于创办人

There is nothing but guide, please use at your own risk. The one who failure in life is the one who followed. Trust your heart.
这是专业的参考手册，滥用后果自负。人生失败者往往都是跟随者。要忠于自己的感觉。

- About Founders 关于创办人

Personal Miles Stone

On the dark side called myself God Father or Underground Theologian, has multiple Criminal Minority, incl. stealth, fraud, fighting, hardcore, gambling and hacking. Deliverance from acute surgery, fatal car accident, stage dismissal, job dismissal, tinnitus, temporary disable, marriage mistake, marriage failure to social blacklisting, a life regret to my ex-girlfriend, in which constituted the reason of writing **Foundation – of End World Backup Plan**, for Crime Syndicate Key Person Disruption.

Aspired in Mechanical Engineering, successfully graduated in Australia Top Tier University regretful defer 1½ year, Coupe with over 12 years Design Engineering skills in R&D Firm Since 2003' Portfolio with over 12 type of **Pillar – CroyalDesign of Machine Gallery**, retired at Forty years old amid apologetic to my Parents. Looking to startup Micro Retail Business as Making a Living for 2nd Part of Career Journey.

Thanks to Wikipedia.com, then founded "**Platform – Light Encyclopedia**" from 2013'-Present, a Light weighted but Comprehensive Encyclopedia (total 700 pages). Hence of the Manual Book, founded Non-profit organization Croyalflush Ministry Foundation Since 2011', progressively building Spiritually Diplomacy Ministry against Villain of Christianity, Rival of Christianity & Cult of Christianity.

On top of that, since childhood has cultured music skills, and then accumulated vast amount of on stage performing experiences in Chinese Orchestra, Folk Music Cafe, and Church Worship Ministry. Impromptu recording include over 21 type of Music Genre published as "**Legacy – CroyalPiano™ Music Encyclopedia**".

Credit to Reformed Church and Fundamentalist Church, was trained as an Apostolic writer for Advanced Theology, Biblical Application to Global Ministry, Author of "**Croyalflush – Fundamental of Christianity**" for Christianity evangelism and reformation website since 2017'.

The Founders included My Parents, Father and Mother, in which involved in Legacy in terms of Inspiration on many topics in this books.

个人里程碑

在黑暗面自称为教父或地下神学家，有多个小型犯罪记录，包括偷窃，欺诈，打架，嫖妓，赌博和骇客。从急性手术、致命车祸、舞台解雇、职场解雇、耳鸣、暂时残废、婚姻错误、婚姻失败到社会黑名单被释放，对前女友来说是一生的遗憾，因此构成了撰写《世界末日备份计划-基础》的原因，即犯罪集团关键人物捣破。

渴望修读机械工程，并成功毕业于澳大利亚顶级大学，遗憾推迟一年半毕业，自 2003 年以来拥有超过十二年在研发公司的设计工程技能，累计荣获超过十二种设计产品奖项里程碑。收录在《石医设计机器画廊-梁柱》，四十岁退休的我对父母道歉。展望于我的微商零售生意当作后半生的职场生涯。

感谢 WIKIPEDIA.COM，从 2013 年至今创立了《活石光百科全书-平台》，轻量但全方位综合百科全书（共七百页）。因这本秘笈书，成立了活石事工基金会始于二零一一年，渐进的与基督教的反派，基督教的对手，基督教的邪派，建立属灵外交事工。

除此之外，从小学习音乐，并在华乐团、民间音乐咖啡馆和教会崇拜事工积累了大量的舞台演出经验。即兴录音包括超过二十一种类型的音乐曲风，《石医钢琴音乐百科-遗产》。

归功于归正派教会和原教旨主义派教会的培训成为使徒作家，专长于高级神学与全球事工圣经的应用等，自 2017 年，创立了基督教福音派和归正网站，《活石基督教-概论》。

创办人包括我的父母，爸爸和妈妈，参与献出思想启发遗产包括其中在书本出现的多个标题。

Epilogue 后记

This is the second part of the series, including two sections. First, Oriental Blueprint, It meant the Heaven Decryption. The Know-how and Know-why of advancing the civilisation to next level in phase of environment, physical health and resource material.

Another section would bring you to witness what impact and highlights of Quantum Science Era transition Pentecost Science Era which is the 4G to 5G transition Era. Of course the highlights was within and in terms of Religion, Technology, Economics and Ethnicity.

Its an exciting fulfilment of all these efforts, indeed the Heaven Decryption endervour, to push human civilisation, aligns with God will, to highest possible level and to auto pilot stage.

这是这系列第二部分，包括两个层面。一是东方蓝图，意为天启。在环境、身体健康和资源材料方面将文明推进到下一个阶段的技术与原理。

另一部分将带您见证量子科学时代转型五旬节科学时代的影响和亮点，即 4G 到 5G 的转型时代。当然，亮点是在宗教、技术、经济和种族方面。

这是激动人心的实现了这些努力，实际上是天堂解密运动，推动人类文明并符合上帝心意，以至达到可能的高峰和自动导航境界。

Made in the USA
Columbia, SC
19 May 2024

34857505R00067